Robert F. Kennedy

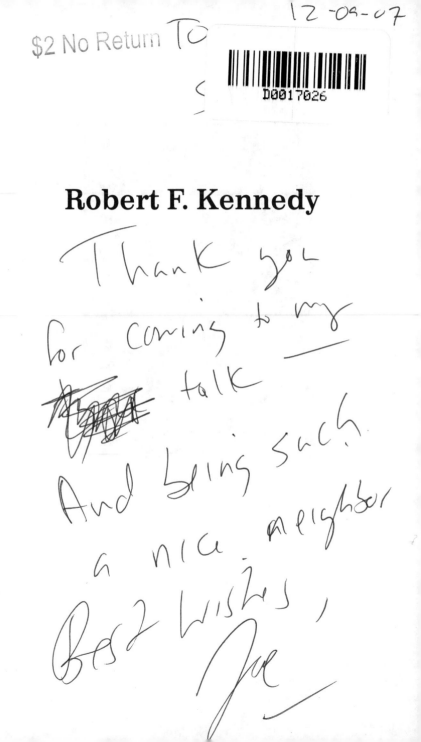

Thank you
for coming to my
talk
And being such
a nice neighbor
Best Wishes,
Joe

Robert F. Kennedy. © Getty Images

Joseph A. Palermo

Robert F. Kennedy
and the Death of American Idealism

THE LIBRARY OF AMERICAN BIOGRAPHY

Edited by Mark C. Carnes

PEARSON
Longman

New York   Boston   San Francisco
London   Toronto   Sydney   Tokyo   Singapore   Madrid
Mexico City   Munich   Paris   Cape Town   Hong Kong   Montreal

Executive Editor: Michael Boezi
Executive Marketing Manager: Sue Westmoreland
Editorial Assistant: Vanessa Gennarelli
Production Coordinator: Scarlett Lindsay
Project Coordination, Text Design, and Electronic Page Makeup:
   GGS Book Services
Cover Design Manager: John Callahan
Cover Photo: © Time & Life Pictures / Getty Images, Inc.
Manufacturing Buyer: Alfred C. Dorsey
Printer and Binder: R.R. Donnelley / Harrisonburg
Cover Printer: Phoenix Color Corporation

Library of Congress Cataloging-in-Publication Data

Palermo, Joseph A.
   Robert F. Kennedy and the death of American idealism / Joseph A.
Palermo—1st ed.
      p. cm.—(The Library of American Biography)
   Includes bibliographical references and index.
   ISBN-13: 978-0-321-38610-6 (alk. paper)
   ISBN-10: 0-321-38610-8 (alk. paper)
   1. Kennedy, Robert F., 1925–1968. 2. Legislators—United States—
Biography. 3. United States. Congress. Senate—Biography. 4. United
States—Politics and government—1945–1989. 5. Massachusetts—
Politics and government—1951– 6. Idealism, American—History—
20th century. I. Title.

E840.8.K4P265 2007
973.922092—dc22
[B]   2007025319

Please visit us at www.ablongman.com

ISBN-13: 978-0-321-38610-6
ISBN-10: 0-321-38610-8

1 2 3 4 5 6 7 8 9 10—DOH —10 09 08 07

For Joseph Nick Palermo,
February 12, 1931–April 2, 2005

Contents

Editor's Preface

Most of the subjects in the *Library of American Biography* series are important presidents, world-shaking inventors, titans of industry, and leaders of social movements. Robert F. Kennedy was none of these. Though he worked in the federal government, culminating in his appointment as attorney general in the administration of his brother, John Fitzgerald Kennedy, few policies are associated with his name. Though a politician, he did not run for high office until he was 38—when he was elected senator for New York. And he died at an age—42—when most of the figures in the *Library of American Biography* series are just coming into prominence.

Why, then, this biography?

Although history is often dominated by those who command center stage, bellowing their message for all to hear, sometimes less visible figures better capture the mood of the nation. Mark Hanna comes to mind, the back-room fixer who shaped national politics during the late nineteenth and early twentieth century, as does Charles Lindbergh, the painfully shy aviator whose solitary feats of courage reflected the aspirations of the American people and whose tragic loss became their own.

Robert Kennedy, as Joseph A. Palermo argues in this inspiring biography, "embodied a spirit of promise and hope" that characterized 1960s America. Robert Kennedy did not acquire iconic status immediately, any more than "1960s America" emerged full-blown on New Year's Day of 1960. During the previous decade, young Bobby mirrored a very different national sensibility: that of a stalwart Cold Warrior and a relentless foe of organized crime.

But Robert Kennedy changed, as did the nation, during the 1960s. He supported the civil rights movement, at considerable political peril to his brother's standing within a divided Democratic

Party. As the world lurched toward a nuclear Armageddon after the Soviets sneaked nuclear missiles into Cuba in 1962, Robert's was the first voice counseling negotiation. After JFK's tragic death by assassination in 1963, Robert embraced antipoverty and civil rights campaigns and became a leader in the movement to end the Vietnam War. Through it all, he conveyed a youthful exuberance and optimism that constitute the most appealing hallmarks of that boisterous decade.

Biographer Palermo, who is also the author *of In His Own Right: The Political Odyssey of Senator Robert F. Kennedy* (Columbia University Press, 2001), emphasizes Robert Kennedy's capacity to inspire grassroots activists and tap into their own enthusiasm. Palermo knows this from personal experience. In 1968 the nine-year-old Palermo had cheered when Robert Kennedy won the California primary—a huge step along his road to the White House. But Palermo's exhilaration was cut short a few moments later by an assassin's bullets. "Hundreds of times I have seen the footage of Kennedy stepping from the podium at the Ambassador Hotel—I show it to my students—and every time I want to jump into the frame, grab him by the hand, and lead him away from the impending abyss," Palermo writes. Robert Kennedy perished, but this book is proof of the enduring power of his life.

MARK C. CARNES

Acknowledgments

This book evolved from a meeting I had with Longman editor Michael Boezi at the 2005 conference of the Organization of American Historians in San Jose, California. At the time my father was in an intensive care unit at a San Jose hospital recovering from a recent medical procedure. When I returned to our family home after meeting with Michael, I learned that my father had passed away that same afternoon. This work is dedicated to my dad.

I am grateful to my colleague Barbara Keys, who introduced me to Jules Tygiel, author of the biography of Ronald Reagan for this series. She had invited Professor Tygiel to give a guest lecture to the History Department at California State University, Sacramento. Over dinner I expressed an interest in writing a book on Robert F. Kennedy, and Professor Tygiel put me in touch with Longman.

I would like to give special thanks to Michael Boezi for all of his help in getting me started on this project. I deeply appreciate his encouragement and guidance. I also greatly appreciate the insightful comments Mark Carnes provided to me early on in the writing process, which led me to reevaluate some of the material I had initially left out of the manuscript. I owe a great deal to Vanessa Gennarelli and Sheralyn Goldbecker for their skilled copyediting, and Saraswathi Muralidhar of GGS Book Services for overseeing production of this book. I am also most appreciative of the time and effort that the following reviewers expended in reading early drafts of the manuscript: Derek Catsam, University of Texas of the Permian Basin; Jacqueline M. Cavalier, Community College of Allegheny County; John Giggie, University of Texas at San Antonio; Larry Grubbs, University of Georgia; John Krueckeberg, Plymouth State University; Peter Levy, York College; John B. Reid, Truckee Meadows Community College; David E. Woodard, Concordia University,

St. Paul. These readers helped me enormously with structure and style. Their comments were invaluable in helping me see things I had overlooked.

I wish to express my gratitude to the History Department of Cornell University for giving me the opportunity to return to Ithaca and to teach a course as a visiting assistant professor in the summer of 2005. I was able to discuss this project with a few of my mentors, including Richard Polenberg and Walter LaFeber, before hunkering down at a carrel in Olin Library to begin my research.

I would also like to thank Jeffrey Buchanan and everyone at the Robert F. Kennedy Memorial Foundation for their assistance. In November 2005 the Robert F. Kennedy Memorial Foundation invited me to come to Washington, D.C., to be one of the guest speakers at the 80th birthday celebration of Robert Kennedy's life. It was a wonderful experience that deepened my understanding of Kennedy's legacy at a time when I had just begun writing this book.

Since joining the faculty of California State University, Sacramento, in 2002, I have taught courses on the 1960s, the Vietnam War, foreign relations, historiography, and the history and politics of the twentieth century. I would like to thank all of my students and colleagues for providing me with a supportive, rich, and diverse learning environment. The history courses at CSUS helped me formulate and refine my evolving views of the 1960s and Robert Kennedy's place within that crucial decade. I thank Professor Chris Castaneda, Chair of the History Department, for helping me construct a schedule of courses that accent my core intellectual interests, which helped immensely with this project. And I wish to give a special thanks to Professor Stan Oden of the Government Department for our lively discussions on all topics relating to the 1960s, and for his camaraderie in the constant struggles of the California Faculty Association.

My mother, Lorayne Mary Palermo, is most deserving of hearty thanks for being truly generous and supportive of me throughout my often difficult academic career. Her courage as a cancer survivor has been a powerful inspiration to me.

Finally, I would like to express my deepest love and appreciation to my wife and companion, Jannette Dayton Palermo, who helped me in a million different ways to complete this project.

Joseph A. Palermo

Introduction

On March 16, 1968, on a crisp Saturday morning in Washington, D.C., Senator Robert F. Kennedy entered the chandeliered caucus room in the Old Senate Office Building, which was filled with his Senate colleagues and their staffs, members of the Washington press corps, his wife Ethel, and nine of their ten children. In an atmosphere of intense anticipation, Kennedy opened his remarks: "I am announcing today my candidacy for the presidency of the United States." He was going to challenge the incumbent President from his own party, Lyndon B. Johnson, for the Democratic nomination. One of the reasons he was running, he said, was to end the war in Vietnam, which had dragged on inconclusively for three years.

On the other side of the world, in Vietnam's Quang Ngai province, American soldiers of Charlie Company under the command of Lieutenant William Calley had gunned down over four hundred men, women, and children near the tiny hamlet of My Lai. Although the My Lai massacre was not publicly exposed for another 20 months, these two events occurring on the same day—one in a distant land, illustrating the growing depravity of an unpopular war, and the other in the nation's capital, pointing the way toward possibly stopping it—marked the parameters of the polarizing, yet idealistic tenor of America in the 1960s. Robert Francis Kennedy embodied the spirit of promise and hope that characterized the period.

Kennedy used his candidacy to broaden the political debate and to confront the multiple crises that engulfed the nation. "I run to seek new policies," he said, "policies to end the bloodshed in Vietnam and in our cities; policies to close the gaps that now exist between black and white, between rich and poor, between young and old in this country and the rest of the world." What was at stake, he said, was the "moral leadership of this planet." His presidential campaign lasted 85 days and ended tragically with his assassination at the age of 42.

Robert Kennedy's personal evolution from a dedicated Cold Warrior to a thoughtful critic of social injustice and an advocate for peace reveals his capacity to learn and to grow. Through understanding his life and the direction in which he wished to lead the nation, we might better understand the profound changes in American society and politics that took place during his lifetime as well as in the decades since his death on June 6, 1968.

Kennedy grew up in a family with a father who had worked for President Franklin D. Roosevelt, and he was exposed at a young age to the foundations of New Deal liberalism. He believed in the central role of government in shaping a more egalitarian society. He came from a wealthy family, and his parents instilled in him the sense that he was obligated to help those who were less fortunate. Kennedy also drew from his moral upbringing a pronounced sense of "good" and "evil" that found expression in the battles he chose to fight; his dualistic worldview would either help him or hurt him depending on the context. He functioned best when his thoughts and actions were in alignment.

After graduating from Harvard and earning a law degree from the University of Virginia, Robert Kennedy's first job in Washington was as a junior counsel on the staff of the Senate's Permanent Investigations Subcommittee, headed by the anti-Communist senator from Wisconsin, Joseph McCarthy. As a young man, Kennedy, like many other Americans, had identified Communism as an "evil" threat, and he believed that the demagogic McCarthy was working to stop its spread. His brief association with the discredited Republican dogged him for the rest of his career. Kennedy subsequently redeemed himself with his work as the lead counsel for another Senate committee, chaired by the Democratic senator from Arkansas, John McClellan, which focused on exposing corruption in the nation's labor unions. His investigations for the McClellan Committee targeted Jimmy Hoffa, the president of the Teamsters, who became a kind of nemesis to Kennedy. Kennedy's pursuit of corrupt labor officials created ill will among some unionists, but his work on the committee was central to establishing his career in government. Kennedy soon secured a reputation for being a tenacious and incorruptible public servant.

Robert Kennedy also played a pivotal role in managing John Kennedy's campaigns, including his 1952 Senate campaign in Massachusetts and his razor-thin victory in the presidential race of 1960. After President Kennedy appointed him attorney general, he became a key player in all of the momentous events of the early 1960s. He again displayed his dualistic worldview by identifying Cuba's Communist leader, Fidel Castro, as an "evil" force and plotting his overthrow. But Kennedy became more aware of the evils of racism in America when he provided federal protection for the "freedom riders" who challenged racial segregation in the interstate transportation system. He also stringently enforced the federal court orders that integrated the Universities of Mississippi and Alabama. As the Kennedy administration matured, Attorney General Kennedy began to see the world in more nuanced terms. He served as President Kennedy's secret envoy to the Russians during the Cuban missile crisis, and he played a pivotal role in defusing the nuclear showdown, which, if mishandled, could have annihilated millions of people. And behind the scenes, he helped to plan the March on Washington, where Martin Luther King, Jr., delivered his iconic "I have a dream" speech. Robert Kennedy was President Kennedy's essential confidante and troubleshooter during the thousand days of his presidency.

With every fiber of his being, Robert Kennedy had served his older brother's public career with a forceful mixture of family loyalty and political conviction. In his early years, he so aggressively promoted John Kennedy's interests that he earned the reputation for being "ruthless" in his single-minded pursuit of tactical advantage. After President Kennedy was assassinated on November 22, 1963, Robert Kennedy was cast into the political wilderness, but he gradually found his own voice in national affairs. The following year he won a Senate seat from New York, and his often dexterous maneuvering through the complex political environment of the mid-1960s illustrated his potential as a leader in his own right.

As senator, Kennedy sometimes wavered on what to do about the war in Vietnam; he could be indecisive, overly cautious, and concerned about his own political survival. But he showed a willingness to take courageous stands when the moment called for them and to challenge others with his own sense of moral outrage against racism, poverty, and the war. In 1968, against long odds, Kennedy bet his political future on an outpouring of citizen activism to attempt to win the presidency and to move the country in a new direction. In his final months, he showed that American democracy worked best when it was energized from below. Through studying Robert Kennedy's words and actions, his capacity to remake himself, and his willingness to fight for his firmly held beliefs, we may deepen our understanding of America in the mid–twentieth century and our ability to evaluate the pained trajectory of liberalism and partisan politics in the decades since his death.

1

Coming of Age

By the mid–nineteenth century, the harsh system of colonial control England had imposed on Ireland created the social conditions that caused a mass exodus of tens of thousands of people. In the late 1840s, the "potato famine" led Robert Kennedy's great-grandfather Patrick Kennedy to leave Dunganstown, County Wexford, to seek a better life in the United States. When Patrick Kennedy arrived in the United States in 1849, Boston greeted him with signs in shop windows reading "No Irish Need Apply." He worked as a barrel maker and in other trades, married Bridgett Murphy, and died of cholera in 1858. That same year Patrick and Bridgett produced one son, Patrick Joseph Kennedy. It marked the beginning of the Irish-American side of the Kennedy family.

P. J. Kennedy, Robert Kennedy's paternal grandfather, grew up in Irish East Boston, labored as a dockhand, and eventually became a successful saloon owner, liquor importer, and politician. He served five terms in the Massachusetts legislature, thus initiating the family's engagement in politics. Although he was not as prosperous as those among the Boston Brahmin elite, by the time he married Mary Augusta Hickey in 1887, P. J. Kennedy had attained a comfortable, upper-middle-class way of life. The couple produced one son, Joseph Patrick Kennedy, who was born on September 6, 1888. He had far greater opportunities for education and advancement than did his parents or grandparents, and he secured similar opportunities for his nine children, including Robert Kennedy. This immigrant story is not unlike thousands of others, but by the middle of the twentieth century, the Kennedy family had come to symbolize the promise and possibilities America had to offer.

P. J. Kennedy was able to send young Joseph Kennedy to the elite Boston Latin School and then to Harvard College. Affluent Protestant Bostonians sent their progeny to Harvard, where Irish Catholic students at that time were a novelty. In 1912, Joseph Kennedy graduated from Harvard and took an executive position with Columbia Trust, a small bank in East Boston that catered to the Irish-American middle class.

In Boston, the 24-year-old Joseph Kennedy inherited many social connections from his father, who knew all of the central personalities in what was a bare-knuckled political environment. Through these contacts, he became an assistant bank examiner for the Commonwealth of Massachusetts. In his government job, the young go-getter learned the intricacies of business and finance and began his lifelong love affair with accumulating money. At the age of 25, Kennedy took over Columbia Trust after rescuing it from near bankruptcy, which made him one of the youngest bank presidents in the nation. The bank had been an important resource in Boston, and his position as its president put him in good stead with the local power structure.

While his family spent summers in Orchard Beach, Maine, Joseph Kennedy became interested in a young woman whose family also vacationed there. Rose Elizabeth Fitzgerald was the debutante daughter of John Francis "Honey Fitz" Fitzgerald. Honey Fitz had served in the state legislature (briefly alongside P. J. Kennedy) and had been elected to three terms in the U.S. House of Representatives. The energetic and gregarious Honey Fitz had built his constituency among the North End immigrant communities, and he was a product of Boston politics, where patronage and money lubricated the party machine. In 1905, he was elected mayor. Initially, Honey Fitz believed his daughter was selling herself short by spending time with Joe Kennedy. He tried to nip their budding romance by sending Rose, his oldest of six children, to convents in New York and the Netherlands.

Rose Fitzgerald was devout in her Catholic faith. At the cloisters in Europe, she was a disciplined student, learning to speak French and German. Yet her absence from Boston did not quell her longing to be with Kennedy. In the end, Honey Fitz had no choice but to capitulate to his daughter's wishes. On October 7, 1914, Joseph Kennedy, 26, and Rose Fitzgerald, 24, were married in Boston by William Cardinal O'Connell.

The couple established a household in upscale Brookline, Massachusetts, a Yankee Protestant neighborhood. In addition to being heralded as one of the nation's youngest bank presidents, Kennedy maneuvered himself onto the board of the Massachusetts Electric Company. He kept track of the political world that his father and father-in-law knew so well, but at that time, he viewed politics as merely another vehicle for the acquisition of wealth. Joseph and Rose produced two boys in quick succession: Joseph Patrick Kennedy, Jr., was born in 1915, and John Fitzgerald Kennedy was born in 1917.

In April 1917, when the United States entered the First World War, Joseph Kennedy became assistant general manager of the Bethlehem Shipyards at Fore River in South Boston. His work with the shipyard led him to cross paths with Assistant Secretary of the Navy Franklin Delano Roosevelt (FDR). A quirky political alliance was born between Roosevelt, the public servant, and Kennedy, the wheeler-dealer, that would last until 1940. "Roosevelt was the hardest trader I'd ever run up against," Kennedy said.

In the early 1920s, Kennedy joined the investment banking house of Hayden, Stone and Company, where he became known as a bold investor. The unregulated stock market meant that cunning speculators could get away with almost anything. One practice in which Kennedy participated was called "stock churning." A handful of big investors would conspire to purchase a targeted stock, thereby increasing its value, only to dump it in concert when it reached its maximum price, leaving less-experienced investors holding the bag. Stock churning and "insider trading" were perfectly legal techniques in the laissez-faire era of Republican Party governance. Presidents Warren Harding, Calvin Coolidge, and Herbert Hoover, aided by their party's control of both chambers of Congress, were among the most pro-business Presidents in American history. "The business of America is business," Coolidge famously declared.

Joseph Kennedy flourished in the freewheeling economic climate of the 1920s. In addition to his stock trading and investment banking, he was caught up in dozens of business enterprises, including the emergent motion picture industry in Hollywood. At a time when the 18th Amendment to the U.S. Constitution banned the sale or consumption of alcohol, Kennedy took advantage of the high prices of liquor on the black market by opening a company that specialized in trading Scotch whiskey. Bootlegging was a lucrative enterprise for the young entrepreneur. (Later, when Prohibition was repealed, he was poised to make another fortune meeting the pent-up demand for spirits.) By the end of the 1920s, Kennedy had become a millionaire several times over, and his driving passion was to create a $1 million trust fund for each of his children. The Protestant elite in Boston still shunned wealthy Irish Catholics, and Kennedy wished to prove that, if he had enough money, even the "blue bloods" would have to accept his family into their exclusive world.

On November 20, 1925, in the middle of the "Roaring Twenties," an era of speakeasies, jazz, Hollywood heartthrobs, and Prohibition, Robert Francis Kennedy was born in the Kennedys' 12-room house in Brookline. He was the seventh child, and his arrival followed the birth of four girls, Rosemary (1918), Kathleen (1920), Eunice (1921), and Patricia (1924). When Robert was two years old, the family moved to New York City to be closer to the center of Joseph Kennedy's expanding empire. They moved into a Georgian mansion built on five acres in Bronxville. Robert's younger sister and brother, Jean and Edward, were born there in 1928 and 1932, respectively. Robert was ten years younger than his eldest brother, Joe Jr., and eight years younger than John. His father focused his ambitions on his two eldest sons, which led Robert to constantly seek ways to gain his father's notice.

When Robert was a young child, the family purchased a vacation home close to Nantucket Sound in Hyannis Port, Massachusetts, and then later a Spanish-style villa for use during the winter months in Palm Beach, Florida. Whether at Hyannis Port or Palm Beach, Joseph and Rose Kennedy emphasized hearty activity for their nine children and valued obedience, punctuality, discipline, and competition. During the summers, the Kennedys drew up daily schedules of activities for their children, assisted by hired help. A typical routine for the children included breakfast at 8:00, followed by an hour each of tennis, touch football, and basketball, then lunch, a rest time, a sailing race in the afternoon, and a swimming period. The large, close-knit Irish Catholic family pursued work and play with equal vigor; idleness was not tolerated. "We were to try harder than anyone else," Robert Kennedy recalled. "We might not be the best, and none of us were, but we were to make the effort to be the best."

If Robert or any of the children was even one minute late sitting down to a meal, it was sure to bring their father's wrath. Joseph Kennedy expected his children, especially Joe Jr. and John, to be conversant in current events, politics, history, and other topics and to lead discussions at the table. Robert was too young to participate in these conversations, but he soon emerged as the most dutiful and obedient of the Kennedy children. Robert's sister Jean recalled how their mother used to worry about Robert "because there were four girls ahead of him, so much competition from the older brothers, and he was accident prone." At one family gathering, four-year-old Bobby rushed to make it to dinner only to crash through a glass door and cut his head. Another time, as a young child, he was so eager to show his older brothers he could swim that he hurled himself off a yawl into the choppy waters of Nantucket Sound. Joe Jr. had to fish him out. "It showed either a lot of guts, or no sense at all, depending on how you looked at it," John Kennedy said.

The family relocated several times while Robert was young. "What I remember most vividly about growing up," Kennedy said later, "was going to a lot of schools, always having to make new friends, and that I was awkward. I dropped things and fell down all the time. I had to go to the hospital a few times for stitches in my head and leg. And I was pretty quiet most of the time. And I didn't mind being alone." Whether entering a new school or interacting with his siblings, Robert constantly tried to win acceptance from the other children. It was difficult for the excitable younger boy with the slight build, wispy hair, and freckled face to be noticed.

Some of his siblings were detached in their religious faith, but Robert followed his devout mother, who embraced her Catholicism without questioning or analyzing. On April 30, 1933, Robert received his first communion, and he became an altar boy at Saint Joseph's Roman Catholic Church in Bronxville. Robert's sisters recalled how hard he had worked at learning his Latin prayers as a boy. Catholicism would be a source of sustenance and stability for Kennedy throughout his life.

Being the son of a self-made millionaire, Robert enjoyed a privileged upbringing. Joseph Kennedy had achieved his goal to build up a $1 million trust fund for each of his children, which was an enormous amount of money in the 1920s. Robert was accustomed to having servants; traveling first-class on trains and ships, including private train cars; and even enjoying the luxury of a chauffeur-driven Rolls Royce. Although later in his life he became an advocate for the poor, Robert as a youth had little understanding of poverty.

By the late 1920s, the U.S. economy began showing signs of strain. The heyday of wild stock speculation had reached its zenith. The market for consumer durable goods had become saturated as most middle-class families exhausted their purchasing power. A crisis in agriculture developed, which was caused by overcapacity after supplying nearly all of Europe with food during the First World War and by a series of dust storms in the Midwest that destroyed millions of acres of farmland. The federal government, under the domination of the Republican Party, failed to heed the economic warning signs, choosing instead to point to the growing value of Wall Street stocks as the key indicator that the economy was doing fine. Soon reality trumped the laissez-faire philosophy as unit banks linked to agriculture failed throughout the Farm Belt and the margin lending for stocks reached its limits. A few knowledgeable investors, including Joseph Kennedy, understood that the good times were over.

Joseph Kennedy's talent for investing spared him the calamitous effects of the stock market crash of October 1929 and the onset of the Great Depression. He pulled his money out of the market about a year before it crashed and then shrewdly began purchasing real estate at deflated prices. The violent labor struggles following the collapse of the economy led Kennedy to believe that business elites had brought on themselves their own misery by mismanaging labor relations. He became an early financial backer of New York Governor Franklin Roosevelt in his bid to win the Democratic Party's nomination for President.

During the 1932 presidential campaign, Kennedy became Roosevelt's valued ally among the business class. Kennedy agreed with FDR that quick action by the federal government to stabilize the economy was the only hope of saving the free enterprise system. He chastised business leaders, including many of his high-roller friends such as William Randolph Hearst, saying Roosevelt was going to "save capitalism from the capitalists." Kennedy became FDR's most important liaison to big business at a time when the Republican Party, the National Association of Manufacturers, and other industry and banking interests spent heavily to defeat him.

In March 1933, when Roosevelt was sworn in as President, Kennedy expected to be appointed to the coveted post of secretary of the treasury. Instead, Roosevelt kept him waiting until 1934 and then asked him to chair the newly created Securities and Exchange Commission (SEC). President Roosevelt's reasoning was that he needed someone who was familiar with the dirty tricks and underhanded dealings of Wall Street to become the federal government's chief enforcer of the new regulations. It was a difficult assignment that won Kennedy no friends in the business community, but he did a superb job cleaning up the enormous, complex mess on Wall Street left over from the crash of 1929 and the bank failures. Kennedy served for 15 months as the nation's top cop on Wall Street, and Roosevelt was pleased with his performance.

During Roosevelt's first term, Kennedy often played host to the President socially at his 25-room mansion in Maryland. Kennedy arranged for Robert to meet President Roosevelt, and they shared their mutual interest in stamp collecting. He urged FDR to write a letter to his nine-year-old boy, and the President obliged, sending Robert some stamps, a handwritten note, and a small philatelist's guidebook. Roosevelt encouraged the child to continue stamp collecting, and Robert framed the note and displayed it in his various offices throughout his life. Even as a youth, Robert Kennedy was constantly exposed to the central tenets of New Deal liberalism and the belief that government was a stabilizing force in the economy and obligated to alleviate America's social ills.

As the 1936 presidential race neared, Joseph Kennedy penned a short book entitled *I'm for Roosevelt*. Robert was not quite 11 years old, but he could see firsthand how his father had become a significant player inside President Roosevelt's administration. Grateful for Kennedy's mass-produced endorsement, FDR sent him a note: "I'm for Kennedy. The book is grand!" That November Roosevelt clobbered his Republican opponent, Alf Landon, in a landslide victory despite big business spending heavily against him. Most wealthy industrialists saw Roosevelt as a traitor to his class, but he had engineered the most significant political realignment of the twentieth century. The Democratic Party became the party of FDR, and the Republicans were shut out of the White House for the next 16 years.

In 1937, Joseph Kennedy still hoped to become secretary of the treasury, but after the U.S. ambassador to the United Kingdom became seriously ill, he asked FDR for the post. President Roosevelt was said to have laughed so hard he nearly fell out of his chair when he thought of sending the abrasive Irish American to the Court of Saint James. He loved the idea and appointed Kennedy to be ambassador to England on December 9, 1937. From that point forward, Kennedy was widely referred to as "the Ambassador." The decision to send Kennedy to England at a time when fascism was sweeping the European continent turned out to be one of FDR's rare lapses of judgment.

On March 15, 1938, 12-year-old Robert—along with his mother; younger brother, Edward; and three of his sisters, Kathleen, Patricia, and Jean—set sail for England aboard the ocean liner *Manhattan* to join his ambassador father. Americans received their first look at young Robert in a newsreel in which he squealed into a microphone at an outdoor press conference: "This is my first trip to Europe and I'm so excited I couldn't even sleep last night!"

In the same month the Kennedys arrived in England, German Chancellor Adolf Hitler launched his *Anschluss* of Austria and made clear his designs on the Sudetenland in Czechoslovakia. Young Robert Kennedy found himself in England at a time of brewing tensions in Europe. Within the year, British Prime Minister Neville Chamberlain attempted to "appease" Hitler (and push him eastward) by assenting to the Third Reich's seizure of the largely German-speaking Sudetenland.

Due to the Great Depression, Britain and France were weak militarily, and their populations were still exhausted from the bloodbath of World War I. Attempting to quench Hitler's thirst for *Lebensraum* ("living space") in Eastern Europe seemed to many observers, including Ambassador Kennedy, the only viable option. Moreover, a militarized Germany was thought to be a useful foil against the threatening power of the Communist Soviet Union. Despite the diplomatic tensions in Europe, for the Kennedy family 1938 had been a magical time; it was a year that Rose recalled fondly for the rest of her life. "This is a helluva long way from East Boston," Kennedy told his wife as they prepared to dine with the Queen of England in Windsor Castle.

For 12-year-old Robert, the move to England made a lasting impression on him. Along with younger brother Edward, he attended Gibbs day school, where he tried his hand at cricket and rugby and got a taste of English sensibilities. Not only did Robert and his family have the opportunity to meet the British Royal Family and Winston Churchill, but also they had a private audience with Pope Pius XII in the Vatican in March 1939.

Ambassador Joseph Kennedy, although an ingenious businessman, betrayed clear limitations as a diplomat. On September 1, 1939, Germany invaded Poland, and Great Britain had little choice but to declare war on the Third Reich two days later. Yet Britain could do little militarily about Hitler's *Blitzkrieg* into Poland. On paper, the two mightiest Western European nations were officially at war. Ambassador Kennedy had phoned President Roosevelt in the middle of the night to inform him of Britain's decision: "It's the end of the world, the end of everything," he sobbed. In late September 1939, Ambassador Kennedy remained in England, but he sent Robert and the rest his family back to the United States aboard the liner *Washington*, which was crammed with some early war refugees.

When Robert returned from England, he discovered that his father had enrolled him in an elite Protestant boys school, Saint Paul's near Concord, New Hampshire. Rose Kennedy, horrified that young

Robert was forced to read a Protestant Bible, overruled the Ambassador and abruptly pulled Robert out of the school. She sent him instead to Portsmouth Priory, a strict Catholic boarding school in Portsmouth, Rhode Island. In this austere Catholic boys school, a place his two rebellious older brothers would have loathed, Robert thrived and embraced his faith along with a disciplined schedule of prayer and study. He enjoyed the structured environment where obeying the rules, studying hard, and praying were mandatory. It gave him much needed stability after attending so many schools. Robert spent two and a half years at Portsmouth Priory at an impressionable age. He began to see the world as a struggle between Good and Evil, and this tendency would be evident in one form or another for the rest of his life.

In England, Ambassador Kennedy uttered damaging public statements. He said Britain would lose the war with Germany and it would be better to accommodate the dictatorships on the Continent. Kennedy's impolitic remarks terminated his working relationship with Roosevelt; but the President chose not to create a political furor by firing Kennedy while Roosevelt sought an unprecedented third term in 1940. Ambassador Kennedy's views were in stark contrast to the united front of the United States and England standing together that FDR wished to project.

Public opinion polls showed that the American people had little interest in jumping into another European conflict, having still not recovered from the bitter experience of World War I. There were also domestic problems, such as high unemployment and poverty, for Americans to worry about, and as a result, there was a strong isolationist sentiment in Congress. Although FDR's New Deal had alleviated the worst suffering, the Great Depression had not lifted. For most Americans, the domestic economic crisis was far more pressing than anything happening on the other side of the Atlantic. Ambassador Kennedy's ideas had weight because at the time most Americans found the isolationist argument more compelling than President Roosevelt's calls for greater U.S. engagement. FDR began bypassing Kennedy in his dealings with the British.

In February 1940, Ambassador Kennedy returned to Washington, and he told reporters that he still believed Germany would be victorious. "Democracy is finished in England," he told the *Boston Globe*, infuriating the British. Kennedy had taken a stand that was antithetical to that of his boss, and right after the election, on November 6, 1940, he resigned, thereby sparing Roosevelt the task of firing him.

At that time, Hitler controlled the European continent and had deployed his state-of-the-art air force, the *Luftwaffe*, to pummel London. Kennedy returned to private business, where he demonstrated greater acumen than in the field of international diplomacy (though he still liked to be called "the Ambassador").

After completing his studies at Portsmouth Priory, 15-year-old Robert entered Milton Academy south of Boston as a junior. The busy Kennedys had no time to give the awkward, skinny teenager a warm send-off. The family chauffeur drove Robert alone to Milton and helped him carry his bags to Forbes House. It was Robert's eighth school in ten years. "The few classmates who recalled anything about him," writes the historian James Hilty, "commented on his Catholic devotion, his almost paralyzing shyness, his sexual prudery, and his all-out efforts in sports."

For Robert, Milton was not an enjoyable place. Being enrolled in many different schools in his youth affected him academically. But he did meet a lifelong friend at Milton, David Hackett. Hackett was a year older, a grade ahead of him, and a "day boy" from a less privileged family. He was also a popular student and star athlete, qualities Robert admired. They became great friends, and Hackett helped Robert adjust. "Nothing came easily for him," Hackett recalled. "What he had was a set of handicaps and a fantastic determination to overcome them." Through enormous effort, Robert became the manager of the Milton hockey team and the vice commodore of the yacht club. By his own account, unlike his older brothers, he was not a sociable teenager with classmates or with the girls.

Three months before Japan attacked the United States at Pearl Harbor Robert witnessed both of his older brothers enlist in the U.S. Navy. His brother Joe began his naval career stationed in Norfolk, Virginia. He once took Robert out on a ride in a Navy plane and even allowed his younger brother to join him in the cockpit (against regulations) to cruise the Atlantic in search of German U-boats. Robert adored his eldest brother, and Joe Jr. looked after Robert. The Navy sent Joe Jr. to England to fly bombing missions, and John became the commander of a PT boat in the South Pacific. Joseph Kennedy, who had dreaded the coming war all along, was proud that both of his sons had enlisted before Pearl Harbor. Robert had just turned 16 when the Japanese raids occurred, and like many boys his age, he was anxious to follow his brothers and serve his country.

In August 1944, Robert came home from Milton to Hyannis Port for a family gathering. He was excited to see John, who had come home after recuperating from spinal injuries in a naval hospital. John Kennedy was still pale and thin and had not yet healed from the wounds he suffered when a Japanese destroyer smashed his PT boat a year earlier. Vivid portrayals of the attack on PT 109 had appeared in the syndicated press, reporting that John, the son of the former ambassador to England, had saved the lives of several of his mates. He had swum for hours towing an injured comrade to a small island where they were later rescued. The Kennedys were proud and happy that "Jack" (which is what they called him) was now safe at home.

On that humid day in August, the Kennedy family sat down to a celebratory lunch that included roasted chicken, ice cream, and blueberries from bushes on their own property. They gathered around a large table on the shaded veranda, overlooking the lawns that stretched to the blue-gray sea. Joseph Kennedy had scheduled a family sailing race for later that afternoon.

But the day was ruined when news came that Joe Jr. was missing in action and presumed dead in Europe. The eldest Kennedy child, feeling competitive with his war-hero younger brother, had volunteered to fly a daredevil mission across the English Channel. He flew a drone "Liberator" bomber loaded with 21,000 pounds of high explosives. The plan was for Joe Jr. and his co-pilot to bail out to a rescue ship and slam the explosive-laden plane into a V–2 rocket-launching site in Normandy. The plane blew up somewhere over the water, killing Joe Jr. and his co-pilot; their remains were never found. Having a son die in World War II was a sacrifice that over 400,000 American families made. For the Kennedys, Joe Jr.'s death was the first of many such tragedies.

Joseph P. Kennedy, Jr., the son for whom his father had planned great things, had vanished in a tremendous blast while on a voluntary mission he did not have to take. Despite the terrible news, a devastated Joseph Kennedy ordered his children to go sailing. Grief stricken, he disappeared into his bedroom. John chose to defy his father. He refused to go sailing. Instead, he walked alone along the waterfront, possibly coming to terms with the fact that he was now the eldest son and all of his father's ambitions fell on his shoulders. Eighteen-year-old Robert, who had looked up to Joe Jr. as only a younger brother can, must have been shattered. Yet he displayed his characteristic obedience by dutifully sailing for the rest of the afternoon, just as his father had instructed. Joe Jr.'s death changed everything for young Robert. He was now the second eldest Kennedy boy, and he would have to help John in whatever ways he could.

2

Launching a Public Life

When Joe Jr. was killed in the war, Robert Kennedy acquired a new set of familial responsibilities and obligations. He longed to be included in the discussions of history and current events that had been central to his father's relationship with his older brothers. "I wish Dad," Robert wrote, "that you would write me a letter as you used to Joe and Jack about what you think about the different political events and the war as I'd like to understand what's going on better than I do now." Joseph Kennedy obliged his 18-year-old son's request, sending him a detailed two-page, single-spaced reply, outlining his views on foreign relations and domestic politics. Robert was proud that his father was beginning to pay attention to him, and he was determined to work hard to win his father's approval as he entered adulthood and began his public career.

In 1940, shortly after Joseph Kennedy resigned as ambassador to England, Robert's older sister Kathleen (nicknamed "Kick"), who was widely admired for her intelligence and spirit, chose to live in London. She soon fell in love with an English nobleman from a stridently Protestant family. On May 6, 1944, with the world still at war, Kathleen and Lord William "Billy" Hartington, the eldest son of the Duke of Devonshire, were quietly married at a London Registry office. Committed to their respective faiths, both families were not thrilled by the union, and Robert followed his mother's lead in silent disapproval. Two weeks after the Kennedys had received word of Joe Jr.'s death over the English Channel, Kathleen learned that a German sniper had felled her new husband while he led an infantry patrol in Belgium. The war had claimed Robert's eldest brother and now a brother-in-law and had landed John in a naval hospital. (Tragically, in 1948, Kathleen was killed in a plane crash in southern France at the age of 28.)

The year 1944, which had brought such suffering to the Kennedy family, was also the year Robert embarked on his studies at Harvard, the alma mater of his father and older brothers. Like so many other young men of his generation, he desired to serve his country before the war ended. "If I don't get the hell out of here soon, I'll die," he wrote David Hackett. Like his brothers, Robert enlisted in the Navy and entered the Naval Reserve Officer's Training Corps at Harvard and Bates College in Maine. He completed his training as the war winded down, and he entered the military as an Apprentice Seaman, Class V-12, Naval Reserve. Joseph Kennedy asked his friend Secretary of the Navy James Forrestal to arrange for Robert to serve on a newly commissioned vessel named after his deceased brother. It was a small request the Navy granted without hesitation.

On February 1, 1946, Kennedy joined the crew of the *Joseph P. Kennedy, Jr.*, a 2,200-ton destroyer, on its shakedown voyage. A photograph appeared in the *Boston Globe* showing Robert being sworn in with his father beaming by his side. When Lieutenant John Kennedy, who was convalescing once again in a naval hospital, received the clipping in the mail, he teased his younger brother in a letter: "The sight of you up there, just as a boy, was really moving particularly as a close examination showed that you had my checked London coat on. I'd like to know what the hell I'm doing out here, while you go stroking around in my drape coat." John's chiding revealed an emerging bond between the brothers that had been rarely expressed.

Until his honorable discharge on May 30, 1946, Kennedy cruised the Caribbean as a low-ranking seaman, scrubbing decks, chipping paint, and standing watch for a nonexistent enemy. He was frustrated that he had missed the war. "I was on a ship named for my brother, sailing the placid waters, and watching beautiful sunsets," he recalled. "Jack had been a hero. Joe had died a hero. Okay, I didn't especially want to be a hero, but it was galling not to have seen any action at all." He had an overwhelming desire to prove that his dedication to defending his country ran as deeply as his brothers' dedication did.

After losing Joe Jr., Joseph Kennedy transferred his boundless political ambitions squarely onto John's shoulders. He goaded his detached 29-year-old son to run for the congressional seat representing

Massachusetts's 11th District. Robert Kennedy received his baptism into the world of politics during John's 1946 bid for the House of Representatives. The elder Boston pols, who operated in the same circles as Robert's father and maternal grandfather, "Honey Fitz," suggested that the untested 20-year-old "Bobby" be sent to work for the campaign in an area where he couldn't do too much harm. His task was to get out the vote in East Cambridge, a rugged, working-class area predicted to vote against John in the Democratic primary by a 5-to-1 margin.

Robert threw himself into the family's political project, canvassing the neighborhoods with no hope of winning. His work ethic and painstaking organizing illustrated his devotion to his brother's cause. After Robert labored intensely for the campaign, playing ball with poor kids in the streets, knocking on doors, and talking to people who greeted a millionaire's son with suspicion, John, as predicted, still lost East Cambridge. But to the surprise of the old pros, Robert had trimmed the expected loss to a 2-to-1 margin. John was victorious in the primary, and in November, he trounced his Republican opponent, Lester Bowen, in the staunchly Democratic district. The political team of John and Robert Kennedy was in its primordial form.

The 1946 campaign was the origin of another vital team that would change Robert Kennedy's life. Ethel Skakel was the roommate of Robert's younger sister, Jean, at the Manhattanville College of the Sacred Heart, a Catholic women's college in Morningside Heights, New York, where the curriculum was laden with self-discipline and prayer. She came to Boston to work as a volunteer to help her best friend's brother win election to Congress. Born on April 11, 1928, in Chicago, Ethel was the sixth of seven children. A vivacious and dynamic girl, she was a competitive horse rider and won scores of trophies and ribbons (some of her more impressive victories were covered in *The New York Times*). The Skakels were a large, successful, and rambunctious family, surrounded by a cacophony of dogs, horses, and other animals and similar in attitude and demeanor to the Kennedys. Ethel was also known for her zany sense of humor, her "inextinguishable gaiety," and her penchant for playing practical jokes on unsuspecting friends and relatives. Her energetic and aggressive spirit was a good match for Robert Kennedy. Her gregarious demeanor brought him out of his often paralyzing shyness.

Like Joseph Kennedy, George Skakel, Ethel's father, was a self-made millionaire who joked that his two favorite hobbies were "old money and new money." He restructured a Chicago coal company into a highly profitable conglomerate, and like Joseph Kennedy, he moved his family to the vicinity of New York City to be closer to the financial action. Unlike the Kennedy patriarch, however, George Skakel had little interest in involving himself in politics.

During the 1946 campaign, Jean Kennedy and Ethel Skakel, who were both 18, were youthful organizers of "Coffee with the Kennedys." "Coffee with the Kennedys" was a tactic whereby the Kennedy women, including the socially sought after matriarch Rose (and as many of the Kennedy sisters as could be rounded up), would rush around from event to event among Bostonian socialites armed with napkins and cups bearing campaign slogans. They provided cookies, pastries, beverages, and Kennedy literature at gatherings, usually held in the private homes of their upscale sisters. (These coffee klatches were so effective that in 1952 during John's run for the Senate, when the Kennedy women were once again deployed, his Republican opponent, Henry Cabot Lodge, Jr., attributed his defeat, in part, to "those damn tea parties!") After John's victory, Robert and Ethel began a tentative courtship. The young couple discovered they had a lot in common, including their deep religious faith and a commitment to liberal politics.

With John's election secured, Robert traveled that summer for the first time to Latin America with family friend Lem Billings. On a purely recreational trip, Kennedy and Billings visited Rio de Janeiro, Montevideo, and Buenos Aires and toured Chile, Peru, Panama, and Mexico. Billings, who had been Jack's sidekick during the wilder years of his youth, noted how puritanical young Robert was on the journey. Unlike his older brother, Robert chose not to try alcohol or tobacco or to carouse while abroad. His goal was to become the only Kennedy son to win his father's promised $2,000 reward for refraining from smoking and drinking before the age of 21. Robert won the prize and bored his traveling companion Billings in the process.

In the fall of 1946, Kennedy resumed his studies at Harvard. Never a stellar student, he focused more on sports. Through hard work and perseverance, he earned a third-string wide receiver spot on the varsity football team. Given his slight build (standing about 5'10" and weighing only 155 pounds), the bulkier players always challenged his gridiron prowess. But teammates recalled Kennedy's gritty determination and viewed him as a highly competitive scrapper and underdog. His attitude on the football field was consistent with what would become his style of political activism. Kenneth O'Donnell, the quarterback of the Harvard team, who, like David Hackett from Milton, became a lifelong friend, tossed Robert a touchdown pass in a game against a low-rated opponent. It was the highlight of Kennedy's football career. His brief appearance in the game against Yale earned him his "letter," of which he was extremely proud; he proved to his father he could attain an honor at Harvard that had eluded both of his older brothers. Touch football, usually pickup games in street clothes, became a form of diversion for Kennedy for the rest of his life. His selfless labors on behalf of John's congressional campaign and his doggedness in sports at Harvard were early indicators of Kennedy's zeal and work ethic, which would become evident in all of his subsequent endeavors.

After the election of President Harry S. Truman in 1948, Republicans began to gain traction with voters by attacking the anti-Communist credentials of Democratic politicians. Democrats, in turn, tried to prove they were just as "tough" on Communism as the Republicans. The Cold War with the Soviet Union and foreign policy generally set the parameters of acceptable debate and shifted the "center" of American politics rightward. The Berlin blockade of 1948, the Soviet atomic bomb test in August 1949, the Chinese Revolution that December, and the outbreak of the Korean War in June 1950 cemented a new bipolar world order. John and Robert Kennedy began their careers at a time when most Americans feared the spread of Communism and saw it as a grave threat to the nation.

In 1948, Robert Kennedy graduated from Harvard without academic distinction, and he and a college friend departed on a trip to Europe and the Middle East. The Ambassador, who urged his sons to learn more about the world through travel, had arranged for Robert to write a series of articles reporting his observations for the *Boston Post*. For a 22-year-old fresh out of college, Kennedy's articles displayed insight and curiosity. In Palestine, he interviewed British officials and Jewish soldiers from the Haganah as well as members of the Irgun, the Israeli terrorist organization that had dynamited a British train and the King David Hotel. He visited a kibbutz and wrote of his admiration of the selfless dedication of its members. At one point, members of the Tel Aviv Haganah picked him up, blindfolded him, and took him to their headquarters to scrutinize his credentials. Kennedy wrote in one article: "The United States and Great Britain before too long a time might well be looking to a Jewish state to preserve a toehold in that part of the world."

Kennedy visited Cairo and went to Athens during the aftermath of the Greek civil war. He was in Italy at a time when the Central Intelligence Agency (CIA) was secretly bribing politicians to block Communist Party gains in the bitter 1948 elections. He briefly toured Germany while the Berlin airlift was in full swing. President Truman supplied the entire population of West Berlin with food and provisions by air in defiance of a Soviet blockade of land traffic. In Belgium, Kennedy visited the grave of his brother-in-law, Billy Hartington. Through Austria, he crossed into the Russian zone of Czechoslovakia while the Soviets were in the process of propping up a client regime there. He returned home via Denmark, Sweden, and Dublin. Even as a young man, Kennedy had a knack for throwing himself into the center of conflicts and learning from his new experiences.

When he returned from his trip, Kennedy gravitated to law school, the natural springboard for a career in government or politics. His grades at Harvard had been insufficient to send him to Harvard Law, so he enrolled in the University of Virginia. In Charlottesville, he studied labor and constitutional law, and he wrote a few papers arguing on behalf of workers' rights. His New Deal ideological roots were evident in the topics he chose to study. As the leader of the Student Legal Forum (his only significant extracurricular activity), he brought an array of guest speakers to the campus. They included Supreme Court Justice William O. Douglas (the Kennedy family friend with whom Robert would later travel to Central Asia); Thurman Arnold (FDR's trust-busting assistant attorney general); James Landis (a member of FDR's brain trust and a Kennedy family lawyer); the anti-Communist senator from Wisconsin, Joseph McCarthy; Representative John F. Kennedy; and, of course, the former ambassador to England, Joseph P. Kennedy.

The most controversial of the visiting lecturers Kennedy invited was the African-American United Nations negotiator Ralph Bunche, winner of the Nobel Peace Prize. In the years before *Brown v. Board of Education* set the precedent for striking down laws separating the races, the University of Virginia was a "whites only" institution, and the city of Charlottesville was racially segregated. After Kennedy invited Bunche to speak, the esteemed diplomat stated that he would not do so before a segregated audience. At one meeting where students balked at signing a petition waiving the rules for Bunche's appearance, Kennedy shouted, "You're all gutless!" The injustice of segregation clearly violated his sense of fair play, and he took his stand against it to the university's governing board. Largely because of Kennedy's efforts, the board agreed to allow Bunche to speak on campus to an integrated audience.

Meantime Robert began seeing more of Ethel Skakel. Jean Kennedy often invited her friend to family gatherings at Hyannis Port and Palm Beach. Ethel's dedication to her Catholic faith could rival even that of Rose Kennedy, and she caused Robert a bit of anguish at one point when she told him she was thinking about becoming a nun. But the couple soon became inseparable. On June 17, 1950, following a lengthy engagement, Robert Kennedy and Ethel Skakel were married at St. Mary's Church in Greenwich, Connecticut. Congressman John F. Kennedy was the best man. Robert was the first of Joseph Kennedy's sons to marry. The reception was a raucous affair, intermingling Robert's athlete buddies, many of whom had gone to Harvard on the G.I. Bill, and the rowdy Skakels, particularly George Jr. who had a well-earned reputation as a practical joker. The groom's ushers were mostly bulky football players of Greek, Italian, and Armenian extraction. The newlyweds spent their two-week honeymoon in Hawaii. On July 4, 1951, Kathleen Hartington Kennedy was born, named for Robert's deceased sister; she was the Kennedy family's first grandchild.

In 1951, Kennedy graduated 56th out of 124 from the University of Virginia Law School. He never entered private practice but took a job in the Justice Department's Criminal Division, where he served briefly under the U.S. attorney for eastern New York. He worked on a few loyalty and security cases, which was his introduction to government investigating. He seemed to be well suited for prosecutorial work where he could harness his unyielding sense of right and wrong.

As the 1952 election year approached, Joseph Kennedy believed that John, who was by now a popular three-term congressman, should seek a U.S. Senate seat. With help from the Ambassador's Boston political allies, labor unions, and hefty amounts of campaign cash, John had a good chance of knocking out Senator Henry Cabot Lodge, Jr., the Republican incumbent. Defeating Lodge would also give the clannish Kennedy family the added satisfaction of bettering a prominent member of the Yankee Brahmin elite. (Joseph Kennedy never felt accepted into the fold of privileged New Englanders no matter how much wealth and status he had accumulated.) But before young Congressman Kennedy could run for the U.S. Senate, the Ambassador believed he needed another trip abroad to expand his knowledge of a rapidly changing world. John invited his brother Robert to go with him on a fact-finding trip to Asia and the Middle East.

Departing in October 1951, the brothers soon found themselves in India attending a dinner with Prime Minister Jawaharlal Nehru, who seemed bored and disinterested with the encounter. Later, in Israel, they attended an event with Congressman Franklin D. Roosevelt, Jr., and they were astounded by his enormous popularity in the new nation. In late October, the brothers were in Saigon, where they got a firsthand look at the U.S.-backed French military bogged down in a war against Vietnamese nationalists. The French-Indochina War (which the Vietnamese called the Nine-Year War of National Resistance) had been raging since 1946, and the French were on their way to defeat at Dien Bien Phu about two years after Kennedy's trip. The Kennedy brothers were dismayed at the quagmire in Vietnam, where over 150,000 French soldiers were attempting to subdue their former colony; they also noted the haughty colonial attitude the French showed toward the Vietnamese. At night, they could hear explosions and small arms fire in Saigon.

The French in Vietnam were "greatly hated" Robert wrote his father, and the American military aid for the war also made the United States "quite unpopular." "It doesn't seem to be a picture with a very bright future," he concluded. John and Robert Kennedy recognized the folly of the French neocolonialist project in Southeast Asia and the difficulty of fighting a guerrilla war in harsh terrain with shaky indigenous support. It was an eye-opening experience that influenced their views of Vietnam for years to come.

While the brothers were on their way to Korea, John became critically ill, and Robert rushed him to a U.S. military hospital in Okinawa. His temperature shot up to a life-threatening 107 degrees. The symptoms were likely a complication of his lifelong struggle with Addison's disease, an adrenal disorder that affects the body's ability to fight infection. The public was told it was malaria. "They thought he would die," Robert later recalled. "Everybody just expected him to die." After a long, emotional night during which Robert prayed by his brother's bedside, John's fever finally broke. He improved rapidly by the next morning. John Kennedy had survived yet another brush with death, and the shared experience in a foreign land strengthened the bond between the brothers. They stayed in Japan for a few days while John recovered and then flew home.

By 1952, the anti-Communist frenzy in America was reaching its zenith. California's Republican senator, Richard Nixon, had used his earlier perch on the House Un-American Activities Committee (HUAC) to become famous for prosecuting State Department official Alger Hiss for perjury relating to espionage. Julius and Ethel Rosenberg were convicted of conspiring to pass nuclear secrets to the Soviets (and were awaiting the electric chair at New York's Sing Sing prison). The HUAC investigated the entertainment industry, hearing testimony from "friendly witnesses," including movie actor Ronald Reagan, and Senator Joseph McCarthy impugned the patriotism and integrity of anyone who disagreed with his notion that the Roosevelt and Truman administrations were guilty of "twenty years of treason."

In preparing for John Kennedy's Senate run, his father, who was a friend of Senator McCarthy's, made a substantial campaign contribution to the Wisconsin Republican with the tacit understanding that he would stay out of Massachusetts and not campaign for Senator Lodge. In 1952, McCarthy's political influence was formidable, and his presence during campaigns could swing the outcome of elections. For example, Joseph Tydings, the Democratic senator from Maryland, was seen as unbeatable, but after McCarthy swept through the state on behalf of his opponent, Tydings lost by over 40,000 votes. "Hell, half my voters in Massachusetts look on McCarthy as a hero," John Kennedy admitted. But the Commie-fighting senator obliged Joseph Kennedy's wishes and stayed out of the state.

During the 1952 Senate campaign, Robert Kennedy displayed his innate management skills. His father had recognized his dedication and work ethic in the 1946 congressional race, and he believed John needed at least one trustworthy confidante as a top adviser. Joseph Kennedy had total faith that his 26-year-old son would be an effective statewide campaign manager. It was the highest office ever sought by a Kennedy, and Robert threw himself into organizing. For the first time, the older, more experienced pols found themselves subordinated to the younger Kennedy. Robert was known as a hard-nosed director. He would drop in unannounced at campaign offices, sometimes throwing out hangers-on and dressing down everybody for not working hard enough to get "Jack" elected.

Massachusetts politicians who had grown accustomed to being coddled as the sources of patronage and favor came to view the younger Kennedy as an abrasive, overbearing, and disrespectful upstart. Massachusetts Governor Paul Dever, a veteran Democrat who was facing reelection, proposed merging the two campaigns but ordered his staff to keep that "young kid" out of his office. "People didn't like me," Robert said later. "But it never bothered me, and I never cared. I mean, it wasn't at all important to me."

For six months, Robert toiled on the campaign, often putting in 18-hour days. He would be the first to open the headquarters early in the morning and the last to leave it late at night. He was constantly breathing down the necks of volunteers and staffers to work harder. It was during the 1952 campaign that Robert Kennedy first earned his "ruthless" nomenclature. He surprised everybody, including John and his father, by displaying colossal organizing abilities that no one knew he had. In the end, John Kennedy defeated Senator Lodge by more than 70,000 votes. (Eisenhower carried the state by 200,000 votes, and Governor Dever lost by 15,000.) Out of the 1952 Senate campaign was born the extraordinary political partnership of John and Robert Kennedy.

But before Robert had the chance to savor his brother's victory, his father challenged him once again: "What are you going to do now?" he asked. "Are you going to sit on your tail end and do nothing now for the rest of your life? You'd better go out and get *a job*." Thus began a short, discontented period of Kennedy's professional life when he felt his talents were not being utilized. Perhaps sensing his son's despair, the Ambassador urged Robert to take a job on the Permanent Investigations Subcommittee of the Senate Government Operations Committee, chaired by his friend Senator Joseph McCarthy.

Foreseeing a potential political maelstrom, Senator-elect John Kennedy urged his brother to forgo the job working under McCarthy. But Robert once again obeyed his father and joined McCarthy's Commie-hunting team. He believed in McCarthy's cause. "At that time," Robert later told a reporter, "I thought there was a serious internal security threat to the United States; I felt at that time that Joe McCarthy seemed to be the only one who was doing anything about it. I was wrong." When Kennedy joined the committee staff, the American people saw McCarthy either as a heroic patriot or as a shameless demagogue. Loathed and loved by millions, McCarthy was famous for his hyperbole about the Communist threat, which he called a "conspiracy so immense, an infamy so black as to dwarf any in the history of man." With great political fanfare, McCarthy's partisan attacks made him a rising star inside the Republican Party (GOP), and as his stock rose, so, too, did that of the GOP. He questioned the patriotism of anyone who failed to see that the United States was "fall[ing] victim to Soviet intrigue from within and Russian military might from without." The publicity he generated catapulted him to a central place in the nation's politics.

It was Robert Kennedy's first job on Capitol Hill. In January 1953, he and Ethel moved to a modest Georgetown home with their daughter, Kathleen, who was 18 months old, and their infant son, Joseph Patrick III, who was born in September 1952. Ethel was already expecting their third child.

On the committee, Kennedy watched as McCarthy turned over most of the investigative work to 25-year-old Columbia Law School wünderkind Roy Cohn, who had made a name for himself doggedly prosecuting the Rosenbergs (who were executed on June 19, 1953). McCarthy put Cohn in command of the entire subcommittee staff of 40 investigators and lawyers, including Kennedy. Cohn gave his closeted lover, G. David Schine, the 25-year-old hotel heir, a plum assignment on the committee. Schine's only qualification was that he had written a tendentious anti-Communist pamphlet, which was placed in the rooms of the hotels his family owned. Kennedy tried to warn McCarthy that he was making a big mistake by putting Cohn in charge, but the senator enjoyed the national media attention Cohn's sensational acts attracted. Kennedy detested Cohn, and Cohn once called Kennedy a "rich bitch" to his face. At one point, the two young men nearly came to blows after a Senate hearing.

In April 1953, Cohn and Schine dashed in and out of ten European cities on a highly publicized junket, at government expense, to remove books they deemed "Communist" from the stacks of the U.S. Information Service libraries. The antics of Cohn and Schine, as Kennedy had predicted, ultimately led to McCarthy's downfall. It began when the U.S. Army drafted Schine for military service and Cohn used his position on the committee to seek preferential treatment for his special friend. Behind the scenes, McCarthy contacted the Army on Schine's behalf, saying he needed him on his staff, not in uniform. When the Army refused to back down and would not give Schine preferential treatment, Cohn began investigating civilian personnel in the Department of the Army for possible Communist ties. In the spring and summer of 1954, Cohn's attacks produced the legendary "Army-McCarthy hearings."

The hearings took place in the Corinthian-columned Senate Caucus Room (the same location where both John and Robert

Kennedy would later announce their presidential bids). The proceedings lasted for 57 days, with 187 hours of live television coverage. The nation was transfixed. At that time, Kennedy had the good fortune to have been recruited to serve as the counsel for the Democratic minority on the committee, and he kept a low profile. His new boss was Senator John McClellan of Arkansas, the ranking Democrat. Kennedy can be seen in footage of the hearings seated behind McClellan at the end of the long table on the Democratic side, occasionally passing a note to one of the senators.

Under the bright television klieg lights, with his typical dramatic flare, McCarthy began to smear the character of a young lawyer associated with the team representing the Army. His accusations led to the culminating event of the hearings when Joseph Welch, the courtly, soft-spoken special counsel for the Army, implored McCarthy: "Let us not assassinate this lad further, Senator. You have done enough. Have you no sense of decency, sir, at long last? Have you left no sense of decency?" After Welch's simple query, McCarthy's game was up. He had stood up to the bullying senator's smear tactics, which he called "recklessly cruel." The American public turned against McCarthy. On December 2, 1954, the full Senate voted 67 to 22 to censure him for behavior "unbecoming" of a senator. (Massachusetts Senator John Kennedy conveniently missed the vote against his family friend because he was in the hospital recuperating from back surgery.)

Senator McClellan assigned Robert Kennedy the task of writing the minority's report. Kennedy impressed McClellan and other senators with his dispassionate, detailed indictment of McCarthy's overreaching. Although he had repudiated McCarthy's tactics in print and the Republicans had abandoned their one-time standard-bearer, Kennedy did not end his personal friendship with the defeated senator. He remained on good terms with McCarthy even as McCarthy suffered his precipitous decline, aggravated by sclerosis of the liver brought on by years of alcoholism. Kennedy often visited McCarthy at Bethesda Naval Hospital. In May 1957, he was one of the few public figures to fly from Washington to attend McCarthy's funeral at Saint Mary's Catholic Church near Appleton, Wisconsin. He still believed that McCarthy's gravest error had been remaining loyal to Cohn. Kennedy was unable or unwilling to grapple with the lasting damage that McCarthy had done to the careers of so many innocent people.

What made Kennedy's relationship with McCarthy more binding was the fact that he was a close family friend. Joseph Kennedy had spent time with McCarthy, and the Irish-Catholic senator had dated two of Kennedy's sisters. He was invited to family gatherings, and Robert Kennedy even asked him to be his eldest child's godfather. McCarthy "was always so nice to me," Kennedy later said. "I never had any personal dispute with him." Although Kennedy authored a highly critical report on McCarthy's management of the committee, at no time during the rise and fall of one of the most notorious senators in American history did he publicly denounce him. "I felt sorry for him," Kennedy said, "particularly in the last year, when he was such a beaten, destroyed person."

When Kennedy resigned from McCarthy's staff, he wrote: "I wish to express to you my appreciation for the opportunity of having served with your group." McCarthy might have been nice to the Kennedys, but to just about everyone else, he was a dreadful bully who coarsened the political debate and created the lasting legacy of "McCarthyism." Kennedy's friendship with McCarthy after the senator had become a pariah illustrates his unyielding loyalty to friends no matter what their misdeeds. Despite the guilt by association that plagued Kennedy for the rest of his life, he learned a great deal about Washington politics serving on the committee that McCarthy had so abused. Kennedy continued to be a staunch anti-Communist; he agreed with McCarthy's goals but disliked his methods.

The midterm elections of 1954 gave control of the Senate to the Democrats, and in January 1955, with the convening of the 84th Congress, Senator McClellan assumed the chairmanship of the Permanent Investigations Subcommittee. He appointed Robert Kennedy chief counsel and staff director. The era of Cohn and McCarthy had ended along with the Republican majority in the Senate. McClellan wished to redeem the hearing process and show the nation that a Senate investigation could be managed efficiently without the kind of bluster and grandstanding associated with McCarthy. McCarthy had pioneered a new style of Senate investigation that was suited for live television, employing high theater, dramatic exchanges, and raw confrontations between prosecutors and witnesses who were under oath. The committee under McClellan's leadership went out of its way to be methodical and professional in examining the alleged criminal or subversive activities of witnesses who were called to testify. He strictly forbade his staff from engaging in speculation and personal attacks during the hearings.

Kennedy, at the age of 29, oversaw a staff of over 40, and he rapidly earned a national reputation as a dogged investigator. After the journalist Charles Bartlett exposed some shady dealings between Secretary of the Air Force Harold Talbot and a few military contracting corporations in which he had a financial stake, Kennedy aggressively pursued the matter. The Talbot case generated positive media coverage for the committee, and Kennedy was widely praised for his professionalism and tenacity in questioning witnesses. The committee unearthed irrefutable evidence of the secretary's wrongdoing, and President Dwight D. Eisenhower asked for his resignation.

Kennedy, who was now living in Georgetown with Ethel and their three children, Kathleen, Joseph III, and Robert Jr. (born in early 1954), had finally reached a place in government service where he believed his talents were valued. Senator John Kennedy, along with his new wife, Jacqueline Bouvier, whom he married in September 1953, often paid visits to Robert and Ethel's home. It was a happy, exciting time for the brothers and their families. The future looked bright for them all. But this tranquil time for Robert and Ethel Kennedy was shattered in October 1955 when Ethel's parents, George and Ann Skakel, were killed in a plane crash. The aircraft, a refurbished B-26 owned by George Skakel's company, exploded in the air over Oklahoma. Kennedy was receiving new lessons in what Arthur Schlesinger, Jr., called the "incertitudes of life."

3

Finding His Way in the 1950s

W hen Congress recessed for the summer of 1955, Kennedy had a reprieve from his work as the chief counsel for the Permanent Investigations Subcommittee. Joseph Kennedy arranged for his 29-year-old son to travel abroad once again. This time he asked his good friend Supreme Court Associate Justice William O. Douglas to take Robert along on his trip to Soviet Central Asia. FDR had appointed Douglas to the High Court in 1939 to succeed Louis Brandeis, and as a jurist, he was known as an advocate for supporting civil rights and protecting public lands. Justice Douglas appreciated the great outdoors, and he was an experienced traveler who had known Robert since he was a boy. He planned to retrace some of the exotic routes that Marco Polo had taken across Afghanistan, Pakistan, India, and Tibet and to enter the Soviet Union from the northern Iranian border. The USSR had gone through enormous changes since the death of Josef Stalin in 1953, and it seemed like a good time for a trip. Robert flew to Paris with his mother and then caught a long flight to Tehran, Iran, where he met up with Douglas. Rose Kennedy sensed that her son was not enthused about the trip. He viewed it more as an obligation to his father than a voluntary adventure. But these kinds of experiences, along with his work serving his brother's political career, deepened Kennedy's understanding of the world and his own emerging role in public affairs.

In Iran, Kennedy and Douglas met with State Department officials and had a brief audience with Shah Reza Pahlavi. (The CIA had enthroned the Shah two years earlier, after orchestrating a coup d'etat against the nationalist Prime Minister Mohammed Mossedegh.) Thus began Kennedy's three-month journey that, as the Ambassador had hoped, opened his eyes to the nuances of life in an "enemy" land. Newsreels of parading weaponry and goose-stepping soldiers in Red Square had forged Kennedy's view of the USSR. Now he learned about Soviet Communism by interacting with ordinary people who lived under its rule. Douglas and Kennedy traveled through the Soviet republics of Turkmenistan, Tajikistan, and Uzbekistan, and local officials greeted them warmly at all their stops. Kennedy hiked for hours and climbed mountains with the adventurous Justice. To his surprise, he learned that, in many parts of Soviet Central Asia, Russian rule had brought an improved standard of living and modernization.

In August 1955, as their tour came to an end, Kennedy and Douglas flew to Omsk, and Robert became ill with a high fever. His attitude toward the Soviets had not completely changed. When Douglas called for a physician to examine him, Kennedy exclaimed: "[N]o communist is going to doctor me!" Douglas forced the issue because he promised Joseph Kennedy he would look after his son on the trip. It took about three hours for a female medical practitioner to arrive. She gave Robert a shot of penicillin and prescribed several days of bed rest. When Kennedy recovered, he and Douglas met Ethel, Jean, and Patricia Kennedy in Moscow. They attended a Russian ballet and toured Leningrad. It was an educational experience for them all to see life behind the "Iron Curtain," especially after years of distrust of the Soviet Union, which Kennedy had internalized. Robert also learned from Douglas a greater appreciation of nature and the value of protecting the environment. The trip, as Joseph Kennedy had intended, broadened his son's worldview by humanizing the people within the Soviet Union.

When he returned home, Kennedy resumed his work on the Permanent Investigations Subcommittee, but he also took on the task of helping his brother's political career. Senator John Kennedy ignored his father's advice and decided to seek the 1956 vice presidential nomination on the ticket that Adlai Stevenson would head. Stevenson was the embodiment of pragmatic liberalism inside the Democratic Party. In 1952, he had run unsuccessfully against General Dwight D. Eisenhower, and he was the front-runner among Democrats for the 1956 nomination. That summer Joseph Kennedy vacationed in southern France, unaware that Robert was canvassing Democratic leaders on John's behalf for the number two slot. Some prominent Democrats, including members of the Americans for Democratic Action (ADA), along with Harry Truman and

Eleanor Roosevelt, were dissatisfied with the young senator from Massachusetts. Mrs. Roosevelt had been the most politically active First Lady in American history, and she was an icon among New Deal liberals. When Senator Kennedy sought her support, she asked him the uncomfortable question of why he had not voted to censure Joseph McCarthy. Mrs. Roosevelt found his answer wavering and unsatisfactory. Although her son Franklin D. Roosevelt, Jr., supported Kennedy, she wanted to discern whether John was cut from the same cloth as his father, whom she detested from the time he was ambassador to England.

On August 17, 1956, at the Democratic National Convention in Chicago, Adlai Stevenson threw open the vice presidential nomination for the assembled delegates to decide. The clear party favorites were Minnesota Senator Hubert Humphrey, who was a liberal stalwart known for championing African-American civil rights, and the two Tennessee senators, Albert Gore and Estes Kefauver, who were among the more forward-looking leaders of the powerful southern wing of the party. On the floor of the convention, Robert Kennedy fought hard for his brother's cause, often aggressively cajoling undecided delegates. Amidst the battle, back at their hotel room, John asked Robert to call their father in France to inform him that he was seeking to join Stevenson's ticket. Kenneth O'Donnell, a close friend of the Kennedys who witnessed the scene, said that everyone in the cramped hotel room could hear Joseph Kennedy shout a string of obscenities on the other end of the line, venting his anger until the phone went dead. Robert hung up the phone: "Whew. Is he mad!"

The next day Robert Kennedy worked tirelessly to create a stampede effect among delegates to support his brother. He moved swiftly around the floor, cutting deals and lobbying hard to win enough votes to put John over the top. He managed to block a win for any candidate on the first ballot, and as the second balloting began, it looked like John Kennedy might be the party's nominee for vice president. There were some moments of high drama until Senator Gore, who was thought to be in the Kennedy camp, threw his support behind his fellow Tennessean, Kefauver. Gore's decision set off a flight away from Kennedy, and Kefauver won the nomination.

John Kennedy's bid to become his party's choice for vice president proved to be a valuable learning experience for his younger brother. Through direct interactions with Democratic power brokers, Robert Kennedy learned about the mechanics of the nominating procedures. He absorbed every lesson and gained firsthand knowledge about how best to curry favor with key players inside the party. He also discovered what kind of incentives worked best with delegates from different states and regions.

Politically, John Kennedy was lucky he lost the nomination. As his father had warned him, Stevenson would be defeated anyway, and party insiders might have blamed Kennedy's Catholicism for dragging down the ticket. Suffering a defeat with Stevenson in 1956 might have tainted his chances of winning the presidential nomination in 1960. Joseph Kennedy saw the vice presidential slot as a "lose-lose" situation for his son. For 30-year-old Robert, his experience of managing John's 1952 Senate campaign and his efforts on the floor of the 1956 Democratic National Convention grounded him in what needed to be done if his brother ever sought the presidential nomination.

After the convention, Senator Kennedy joined his father and brother Edward in southern France for a two-week yacht cruise. He left behind his wife, Jacqueline, who was in her third trimester of a difficult pregnancy and remained with her mother in Newport, Connecticut. On August 23, Jacqueline was rushed to the hospital due to internal bleeding, and doctors performed an emergency cesarean section. The premature baby girl had been stillborn. John Kennedy did not learn of the news until the ship docked in Genoa, Italy. His absence during his wife's traumatic experience became an embarrassment when the press picked up the story. Robert Kennedy rushed from Hyannis Port to Newport to be at Jackie's bedside when she awoke from the operation. He was the one who told her the sad news, and he arranged for the burial. The dutiful younger brother, in addition to being a campaign manager and political operative, found himself in the familial role of providing emotional support for his sister-in-law while his brother frolicked in the Mediterranean.

Following the loss of her first child, Jacqueline Kennedy wanted to move out of the large antebellum home she and John had purchased a year earlier in the rolling hills of McLean, Virginia, called "Hickory Hill." They sold the estate to Robert and Ethel for $125,000, the same price they had paid for it. Hickory Hill was better suited for Robert Kennedy's growing family, with four young children and another one on the way. The large home, with its acres of land and plenty of room for children, horses, and other animals, was well suited for the kind of life Robert and Ethel wished to build together.

In the fall of 1956, Robert's political education continued when Adlai Stevenson asked him to join his presidential campaign staff.

Stevenson asked Kennedy to help him reach out to Catholic voters and to provide general political advice. Arthur Schlesinger, Jr., who was also on Stevenson's staff, remembered Kennedy on the campaign trail as "an alien presence, sullen and rather ominous, looking grim and exuding an atmosphere of bleak disapproval." Kennedy did not like what he saw while he traveled with Stevenson. He believed the campaign held too many meetings and the candidate wasted far too much time honing intricate phrases of his speeches instead of meeting with local Democratic officials and campaign volunteers.

Kennedy was determined to learn from Stevenson's mistakes. He took copious notes on every aspect of the campaign, deploying his skills as an independent observer. He urged Stevenson to speak extemporaneously more often and to make a greater effort to connect with voters. He believed Stevenson's rhetoric was too lofty and his speeches were difficult for ordinary people to follow. He thought the campaign was listless and without a coherent strategy. "Stevenson was just not a man of action at all," he concluded. After spending six weeks on the campaign trail with Stevenson, Kennedy's opinion of the two-time presidential candidate had been "destroyed." He gleaned from the Stevenson experience every bit of knowledge that might help his brother in 1960. He learned what *not* to do if John ever got the nomination. In November, Kennedy cast his vote for Eisenhower.

After Stevenson's defeat, Kennedy returned to Capitol Hill to take on his most weighty federal assignment to date. In January 1957, Senator McClellan chaired a new congressional committee, the Senate Select Committee on Improper Activities in the Labor and Management Field, known in the press as either the "McClellan Committee" or the "Rackets Committee." It was charged with looking into the widespread allegations of graft and corruption in some of the nation's largest labor unions. Three senators from the Permanent Investigations Subcommittee and three from the Labor Committee, including John Kennedy, made up the committee.

McClellan was known as a meticulous and dignified senior senator who had tragically lost two sons in accidents. He was impressed with Robert Kennedy's work for the minority during the McCarthy debacle as well as with his work on trade and procurement issues when McClellan became chairman. He appointed the 31-year-old to be the committee's chief counsel. Under Kennedy's leadership, the McClellan Committee became the most efficient investigative arm then operating on Capitol Hill. It was a demanding job, but McClellan recognized in Kennedy a hard-working enthusiast who possessed extraordinary skills. The fact that Senator Kennedy also served on the committee gave the Kennedy brothers for the first time a high degree of national visibility and positive name recognition. Yet they were walking through a political minefield because their pursuit of corrupt unionists could alienate the Democrats' labor base, which any candidate needed in order to win the party's presidential nomination. It was risky for Democratic politicians to go after corrupt labor bosses, no matter how strong the evidence. Thirty-five percent of the nation's work force belonged to unions, and at the local level, they provided the lifeblood of the Democratic Party, money and volunteers.

Robert Kennedy believed that unions such as the International Brotherhood of Teamsters, which could shut down the nation's ground transportation, if hollowed out by corruption could be a threat to "national security." "We have to be successful [against organized crime] because it can't be any other way," Kennedy told his staff. "Either we are going to be successful or they are going to have the country." The McClellan Committee introduced Kennedy to an army of federal prosecutors and FBI investigators. He hired Kenneth O'Donnell, a Kennedy family friend; Pierre Salinger, a San Francisco journalist; and Walter Sheridan, a former FBI agent, as committee staff. He also brought on board a former head of the FBI's accounting section, Carmine Bellino, who was widely respected as the nation's most skilled investigator of bookkeeping irregularities. It was the first time Kennedy showed his ability to assemble a first-rate staff of idealistic civil servants. He also hired as his executive secretary Angela Novello (Bellino's sister-in-law), who would manage Kennedy's unruly offices for the next 13 years.

The Teamsters caught the attention of the McClellan Committee because newspapers had widely reported alleged criminal activities inside the union. A preliminary investigation, aided by the journalistic digging of dozens of investigative reporters—most notably, Edwin Guthman, who won a Pulitzer Prize for his efforts—revealed illegal operations within the nation's largest transport union. Investigators unearthed evidence that the Teamsters president in Seattle, Dave Beck, a national figure who had been photographed with President Eisenhower, embezzled union funds for his personal enrichment. Kennedy led the McClellan Committee's efforts to investigate Beck, and the Teamsters president was later indicted and convicted. After Beck's downfall, a Teamsters vice president, James Riddle Hoffa, sought to replace him, and the committee began looking into his background. Evidence surfaced that Hoffa, too, had been involved in shady dealings. Thus began a long, bitter professional and personal battle between Robert Kennedy and Jimmy Hoffa.

Hoffa was born in Indiana but grew up in a gritty area of Detroit. His mother moved the family there when Hoffa was a boy, following the death of his father from silicosis, a disease he contracted while he worked as a coal miner. As a youth, Jimmy Hoffa had been a courageous union organizer. He fought strike-breakers and the police, and once he was nearly killed by anti-union goons who whipped him with chains. The short and stocky Hoffa was intelligent and streetwise and possessed an iron will. He neither smoked nor drank, and unlike flashier labor leaders like Dave Beck, Hoffa was indifferent to his wardrobe. He lived modestly and remained a loyal husband to his wife, Josephine. He appeared to be a paragon of virtue, and he was popular among the rank-and-file workers. By the mid-1950s, Hoffa was a power-house inside the Teamsters union. In addition to managing an enormous pension fund, Hoffa controlled numerous "paper locals," which were fake organizations that could "vote" to strengthen his power in the national union. His goal had always been to build up the Teamsters by any means necessary, including eliciting help from organized crime.

Senator McClellan subpoenaed the 44-year-old Hoffa to testify before the committee, and the rugged unionist repeatedly sparred with Kennedy in nationally televised hearings. The public was interested in the unfolding crime story. Kennedy's pointed questions and Hoffa's steely responses created some moments of high drama. Kennedy repeatedly asked Hoffa to clarify threatening statements he had made against his enemies that had been caught on wiretaps: "What did you mean that you were going to 'break his back' Mr. Hoffa?" Kennedy asked. "Just a figure of speech," Hoffa replied tersely, "just a figure of speech." Such exchanges were common as Kennedy tried to pick away at Hoffa's law-abiding veneer. The investigation of Hoffa's racketeering activities was difficult and frustrating for prosecutors. Hoffa and his lawyers shrewdly influenced juries and public opinion, and each time there seemed to be sufficient evidence to bring a conviction, the burly Teamsters leader somehow wriggled out of it.

Federal investigators found that Teamsters' financial records had been destroyed or altered, witnesses had dropped out of sight, and subpoenas were often ignored. While the committee did its work, Kennedy testified to Congress, calling for stricter laws prohibiting the manipulation of union funds. He also advocated opening up the unions' books to the Department of Labor. Robert Kennedy's prosecutorial conduct could be heavy-handed, and he generated ill will among some labor unionists that lingered for the rest of his life.

Kennedy pushed his staff hard, and often his subordinates did not leave the office before midnight. At the peak of its activities, there were 45 legal consultants and 35 investigators working under him, with 20 secretaries and clerks. On the drive home late one night, Kennedy noticed the light burning in Hoffa's attorney's office. He ordered the car turned around: "If he can stay late so can we," he told the unfortunate staffers who happened to be with him. (Hoffa later said he had heard about the episode and began leaving the lights on all night just to taunt Kennedy.)

Kennedy's tenacity earned him the respect of Carmine Bellino, the committee's expert on illegal accounting practices and a 27-year veteran of the FBI, who said: "Bob is the only man I've met in government who is willing to go all the way, all the time." His work was having an effect: Dozens of corrupt union officials lost their jobs, and about a hundred of their associates were sent to prison. Kennedy participated in questioning 1,500 witnesses, many of them during televised hearings. His boyish appearance, distinct nasal voice, and sharp interrogations established him for the first time as a national figure in his own right. Both John and Robert Kennedy participated in some of the hearings, and they gained national media exposure as two young, telegenic, and principled government officials.

In 1960, Robert Kennedy published his first book, *The Enemy Within*, in which he outlined why the nation faced a serious risk from labor union corruption and what kind of citizen action was needed to stop it. "It seems to me imperative that we re-instill in ourselves the toughness and idealism that guided the nation in the past," he wrote. "The paramount interest in self, in material wealth, in security must be replaced by an actual, not just vocal, interest in our country, by a spirit of adventure, a will to fight what is evil, and a desire to serve."

In *The Enemy Within*, Kennedy described trips he took with Bellino to several American cities to uncover corrupt practices in the unions. They found evidence of shakedowns and beatings of rival labor organizers by mob-affiliated unions. Local law enforcement officials told them about a unionist in San Diego who mobilized the city's jukebox operators. Thugs warned him to stay out of the city, but he continued his activities until one night he was beaten unconscious. When he awoke, he suffered from severe abdominal pain. He drove to the nearest hospital where X-rays revealed its source: a cucumber had been lodged in his colon. Emergency surgery was necessary to remove it. Stories such as these shocked Kennedy, who had led a sheltered life far from the routine violence of organized criminals. He became highly motivated in the fight against the new evil he had identified, and he found the challenge dangerous and exhilarating. Threats from mobsters had to be taken seriously. *The New York Herald Tribune* reported that Kennedy had received death threats and anonymous phone calls warning him to stop investigating or acid would be thrown in his children's faces. Publicly, Kennedy denied that he ever received death threats.

In Kennedy's dualistic worldview, Jimmy Hoffa fit into the mold of an "evil" man, and his pursuit of Hoffa became, according to Arthur Schlesinger, "an intensely personal duel." As the investigation unfolded, Kennedy learned that Hoffa offered to bribe John Cheasty, a New York attorney who worked on the committee. Kennedy contacted FBI Director J. Edgar Hoover, who arranged a sting operation where Hoffa would meet with Cheasty to give him a payoff. FBI cameras caught Hoffa handing over an envelope stuffed with cash.

Prior to the sting, Kennedy and Hoffa were both invited to dinner at the home of Eddie Cheyfitz. Cheyfitz was an associate of the Teamsters' attorney, Edward Bennett Williams, whom Kennedy knew well. Kennedy knew Hoffa was spying on the committee, and this face-to-face meeting gave Kennedy the opportunity to see his nemesis up close. From that point on, Kennedy's fight with Hoffa seemed to become a battle of wills. To Hoffa, Kennedy was a "rich kid" who never worked an honest day in his life. To Kennedy, Hoffa was a hoodlum whose ultimate victims were the workers who paid into the Teamsters' pension system.

Kennedy unleashed against Hoffa all of the powers at his disposal with little prosecutorial discretion. He introduced incriminating evidence, asked probing questions, and examined the minutiae of the Teamsters' financing. Hoffa proved an unflappable witness, never exposing himself or making careless mistakes, and all the while glaring at the chief counsel for long periods without blinking.

Kennedy told his aides: "Hoffa has said every man has his price, and you have seen his corruptive influence spread to the leading citizens of the towns across the United States, the leading bankers, the leading businessmen, officials, judges, Congressmen. If he can get them to do his bidding, if he can buy them, then you can see what it means to the country. Either we are going to be successful or he is going to have the country."

In 1957, a jury with which Hoffa had tampered acquitted him of all charges, and his popularity increased among the union's rank and file. Within a year of his acquittal, they elected him national president of the Teamsters. Hoffa had eluded conviction and was sure to outlast the life of the committee. Kennedy had quipped to the press that he was so confident of the Teamsters president's guilt that he would jump off the Capitol dome if Hoffa was not sent to jail. Hoffa's attorney, Edward Bennett Williams, reveled in telling reporters he would provide a parachute to Kennedy if he needed one for the leap. Kennedy's battle with Hoffa entered the appeals process, but it was not over.

Meanwhile Kennedy's family continued to grow, with the birth of David Anthony Kennedy in June 1955 and Mary Courtney Kennedy in September 1956. Ethel had been pregnant during most of the hearings, but it did not stop her from attending. Michael LeMoyne Kennedy was born in February 1958, and Ethel showed up in the hearing room with her newborn baby in her arms. Kerry Kennedy followed in September 1959. The Kennedy family had grown to seven children and counting. In 1960, on Father's Day, Kennedy was named "Father of the Year" by the National Father's Day Committee, which recognized both his achievements in government and the care he took in tending to his large family. But his family obligations extended beyond his wife and children as he prepared to take on the role of John Kennedy's campaign manager when he decided to run for the presidency.

Since the death of Joe Jr., Joseph Kennedy had been grooming John to make a run for the presidency when the timing was right. In 1960, Eisenhower's two terms would be over, and the Republicans would pass the mantle to Vice President Richard Milhous Nixon of California, who was vulnerable. Late in Eisenhower's second term, reporters asked the President if he could recall any significant contributions Nixon had made to his administration. "Give me a couple of weeks and I might be able to think of one" was Ike's reply. It was far from a ringing endorsement.

In April 1959, at a meeting in Palm Beach, Robert Kennedy assumed the role of his brother's campaign manager for the upcoming Democratic primaries, and he assigned the inner circle of advisers with their tasks. Augmenting the Kennedy team, which included the pivotal in-laws, Sargent Shriver and Stephen Smith, he brought on board Pierre Salinger and Walter Sheridan from the McClellan Committee. Kenneth O'Donnell and David Hackett came to help, along with two intellectuals, Richard Goodwin and Theodore Sorensen, who became speechwriters. As he had done with the Rackets Committee, Kennedy assembled a highly capable staff. "It's ridiculous that more work hasn't been done," he said. "A day lost now can't be picked up on the other end." Kennedy, who was only 33 years old, took on the most demanding job of his life. It was an enormous endeavor that had the potential to alter the course of American history.

Kennedy retained the services of Lou Harris as the campaign's full-time pollster to provide him with raw data on the electorate. Of particular concern was whether or not the American people were ready to elect the nation's first Catholic President. Democratic insiders were hesitant to nominate a Catholic ever since Al Smith was handily defeated in 1928, in part because he was Catholic. John Kennedy handled the religion issue skillfully, but everyone knew that it could cost votes. Of the nation's 180 million citizens in 1960, only about 23 percent indicated in polls that they were Catholic, while 35 percent identified themselves as Protestant. One aim of the campaign was to win back those Democrats who, like Robert Kennedy, had voted for Eisenhower in 1956. In 1960, John Kennedy had three chief rivals for the nomination: Minnesota Senator Hubert Humphrey; Lyndon Johnson, the Senate majority leader from Texas; and Adlai Stevenson, who, even though he had lost the two previous presidential races, still had a die-hard following among liberals in the party.

Against Robert's advice, John chose to enter the Wisconsin primary. It was a two-man race between Kennedy and Humphrey, who had the advantages of being from a neighboring state and having a solid record on agricultural issues. Wisconsin had a slightly higher number of Catholics than other states in the region, which could help Kennedy, but Robert worried that opponents might exploit the issue. He became incensed when on primary election night Walter Cronkite asked the candidate a question about Catholic voters; he threatened to forbid Cronkite from any further interviews.

In the end, John Kennedy won with 56 percent of the vote, and Humphrey ran an honorable campaign that did not raise Kennedy's Catholicism.

The West Virginia primary followed quickly after Wisconsin, and the Kennedy campaign feared that the religion issue might surface because Catholics made up only about 4 percent of the state's population. Robert Kennedy trudged through West Virginia, shaking hands with coal miners and saying: "My name is Bob Kennedy. My brother is running for President. I want your help." He played on the overwhelming popularity of FDR among West Virginians, who were still grateful for the New Deal programs that brought electrification to the region and bailed them out of the Great Depression. Kennedy brought Franklin D. Roosevelt, Jr., to the state to stump for his brother. In an ecumenical spirit, John Kennedy framed the subject of his religion as one of tolerance versus intolerance. "No one asked me if I were Catholic when I joined the U.S. Navy," he said.

In West Virginia, the Kennedy campaign's publicly disclosed expenses were four times those of Humphrey, and there was evidence of payoffs to voters throughout the state. Behind the scenes, Joseph Kennedy distributed large sums of campaign cash to wavering Democratic officials. These money transfers no doubt gave the Kennedys an enormous advantage and led opponents to charge them with "buying" the election. In the end, John Kennedy beat Hubert Humphrey handily with 61 percent of the vote. However, victories in the primaries did not guarantee a candidate the nomination; delegates would choose the winner at the Democratic National Convention.

Throughout the primary campaigns, Robert Kennedy was at the center of a flurry of activity where he fought hard for every delegate he could corral, cajole, or even threaten into joining his brother's cause. He was single-minded in his pursuit of the nomination. Volunteers were known to quietly utter, "Little Brother is watching" (a play on a line in George Orwell's *1984*), because Robert Kennedy hovered over their every move. RFK, above all else, wanted to win.

In July 1960, at the Democratic National Convention in the Los Angeles Sports Arena, Harris Wofford, who was a civil rights activist and an ally of Martin Luther King, Jr., headed the Kennedy campaign's efforts to reach out to African-American voters. With the help of other liberals, he inserted into the party platform uncompromising language on civil rights that was sure to spark opposition from the segregationist southern wing of the party. Robert Kennedy wanted the support of the party's African-American delegates, who numbered only about 250 out of 4,500 but represented an important bloc of voters in key industrial states.

Consistent with what he had done in law school when he defended Ralph Bunche's right to speak before a racially integrated audience, Kennedy ordered his staff to go "all the way" with the civil rights plank. "Don't fuzz it up," he demanded, saying that there were other reasons southerners would vote for John Kennedy; "don't let there be any doubt anywhere as to how the Kennedy people stand on this." After framing the Catholic issue as one of tolerance, Kennedy saw the hypocrisy in pandering to southern Democrats' proclivities on race to woo segregationists. Robert's hard work paid off; his brother narrowly won the nomination on the first ballot. Right after the voting, the Kennedy brothers could be seen huddling together amidst the crowds on the convention floor; Robert was standing over the candidate "hitting his open palm of his left hand with the fist of his right hand," while John sat listening with a contented smile on his face.

As campaign manager, Robert Kennedy earned the reputation of being brash, pushy, and difficult to get along with. "I'm not running a popularity contest," he told a reporter. "It doesn't matter if they like me or not. Jack can be nice to them. . . . Somebody has to say no. If people are not getting off their behinds and working enough, how do you say that nicely?" The political journalist Murray Kempton wrote: "Whenever you see Bobby Kennedy in public with his brother, he looks as though he showed up for a rumble." With his work for Joseph McCarthy and the McClellan Committee, along with his relentless labors on behalf of his brother, Kennedy's combativeness reinforced his "ruthless" image. He could be a polarizing figure who operated best when his thoughts and actions were in alignment. Winning the White House for his brother in November now became Robert Kennedy's all-consuming passion.

His Brother's Keeper

Robert Kennedy found himself at the center of a series of fierce political battles that would alter both his role in public affairs and the direction of twentieth-century American history. At the 1960 Democratic National Convention, some delegates feared an anti-Catholic backlash if John Kennedy was nominated, while others believed he was too inexperienced. Texas Governor John Connally and other allies of Senate Majority Leader Lyndon Johnson, who also sought the nomination, implied that Kennedy was too unhealthy to be President. Many senior politicians knew that Kennedy was in worse physical condition than he publicly let on. His Addison's disease, which depleted his immune system, required him to receive constant injections of cortisone. Robert Kennedy was extremely sensitive to the public perception of his brother's health. He was furious when he heard that Johnson at one of the caucuses had described John as a "little scrawny fellow with rickets." Johnson also called Joseph Kennedy a "Chamberlain-umbrella policy man" who thought "Hitler was right" and who wanted his son to be President so he could "run the country." "I've seen Bobby mad," Kenneth O'Donnell remarked later, "but never as mad as the day he heard what Johnson said about his father." The bad blood between Robert Kennedy and Lyndon Johnson began at the 1960 convention.

On July 13, 1960, when John F. Kennedy won the presidential nomination, everyone knew the election would be tight, which made his choice of a running mate a crucial decision for the party. Robert Kennedy did not want Lyndon Johnson on his brother's ticket; he preferred Missouri Senator Stuart Symington, whom he knew well from the Permanent Investigations Subcommittee. Among Democrats, Johnson was a power unto himself, and he was already a legendary Senate majority leader. Throughout the 1950s, he was well known for the "Johnson Treatment," whereby he utilized his 6'4" frame to physically intimidate senators to win their votes.

Johnson was second in the balloting, and given his seniority and position, the Kennedys believed a pro forma offer of the vice presidential slot would be a unifying gesture. Given his power in the Senate, they did not think Johnson would accept being number two to a younger, less experienced candidate who had a good chance of losing. To their surprise, Johnson snapped up the offer, which set off confusion in the Kennedy camp. "We changed our mind eight times" about the nomination in a few hours, Robert said, with most of the time spent trying to figure out "how could we get out of it."

It was up to Robert Kennedy, as his brother's emissary, to meet with the domineering Texan to sound out whether he was serious about joining the ticket and whether he might reconsider. Thereafter followed a string of stormy meetings between Kennedy and Johnson. The vice presidential slot had been formally proffered, and to renege on it now would be an early embarrassment for the Kennedy campaign, which needed all of the allies it could get. In the course of 18 uncomfortable hours, the matter was settled: John Kennedy and Lyndon Johnson would be the Democratic Party's 1960 nominees for President and vice president. Later the press called the decision to add Johnson to the ticket a stroke of genius. He helped the Massachusetts senator win votes in the South, and Johnson's role as Senate majority leader rounded out the team with experience and political know-how. But the clumsy handling of the decision was an inauspicious start for the Kennedy/Johnson campaign.

Over the course of the next few months, Robert Kennedy did more to win the presidency for his brother than any other individual. He was ubiquitous in the state and local campaign offices, constantly pushing staffers to work harder. "You can rest in November," he told his underlings. Like earlier campaigns, he utilized the Democratic Party structures where they were reliably pro-Kennedy and turned to the independent Citizens for Kennedy chapters, which were far more nimble, when necessary. Citizens for Kennedy functioned as a grassroots network that mobilized voters at the local level. Robert Kennedy had little concern for the careers of state and local politicians; his single-minded goal was to win the presidency for his brother. When the campaign encountered disagreement from some entrenched Democrats in New York City who were always looking for ways to reap political benefits from the Kennedy machine, Robert Kennedy told them: "Gentlemen, I don't give a damn if the state and county organizations survive after November, and I don't give a damn if you survive. I want to elect John F. Kennedy!"

As anticipated, the religion question reared its head. A few right-wing Protestant clergymen, such as Norman Vincent Peale and Daniel Poling, who formed the National Council of Citizens for Religious Freedom, predicted disaster for the Republic if Kennedy was elected. They feared a Catholic chief executive would hand over the nation to the Vatican. Once again displaying his ecumenical sensibilities, John Kennedy confronted the subject at a campaign appearance before the Greater Houston Ministerial Association, where he emphasized his belief in the separation of church and state. "I am not the Catholic candidate for President," he said. "I am the Democratic Party's candidate for President who happens to be Catholic." As he had done during the West Virginia primary, Kennedy framed the religious question as a test of tolerance. At a campaign rally in Cincinnati, Robert Kennedy's eyes welled with tears when a critic raised the topic: "Did they ask my brother Joe whether he was a Catholic before he was shot down?" he asked.

Robert Kennedy brought the 1960 campaign into the modern era by hiring a mobile videotape crew to follow the candidate. The campaign provided the tapes to local television outlets for broadcast on the same day Kennedy entered a given locale and also used the footage in campaign commercials. According to historian James Hilty, the videotapes were "not only showing the candidate and voters in natural poses and coloring the campaign with a spontaneous quality, but allowing them to customize appeals to specific groups and regions." But the most telling use of television during the campaign was the four debates between John Kennedy and the Republican candidate, Vice President Richard Nixon.

Held on September 25 and October 7, 13, and 21, the Kennedy-Nixon debates reached an estimated 65 million television viewers. John Kennedy had mastered the visual medium and projected the image of a movie star, tanned and relaxed, while Vice President Nixon appeared haggard, excitable, and negative. Nixon refused to wear the thick makeup designed to counter the unflattering effects of the harsh TV lighting, which only accentuated his five o'clock shadow. Offstage before one debate, after the vice president sent away his makeup artist, a Nixon aide asked Robert Kennedy what he thought of Nixon's appearance. "Terrific! Terrific! I wouldn't change a thing," Kennedy replied. Although Nixon had used television to great effect in 1952 when he delivered his famous "Checkers" speech, which rescued his vice presidential candidacy from a corruption scandal, Nixon's handlers could not compete with the Kennedys' favorable use of visual media in 1960.

Percolating just below the surface of national Democratic politics was the schizophrenic nature of the party's North-South regional divide. From the time of the Compromise of 1877, which marked the end of Reconstruction, the state and local governments of the former Confederacy had dedicated themselves to enacting a tapestry of laws that codified racial segregation. By the turn of the century, there emerged the "Solid South," the Democratic Party's most loyal bloc of electoral votes. In the 1930s and 1940s, FDR and Truman were able to win northern African-American voters despite the party's segregationist wing, but the profound divisions persisted.

The Supreme Court's 1954 *Brown v. Board of Education* decision changed the balance by outlawing legal racial segregation in public elementary and secondary schools. A year later Rosa Parks refused to go to the back of the bus in Montgomery, Alabama, thereby igniting a new phase of the African-American civil rights struggle. In February 1960, black college students jumped into the fray and began using nonviolent civil disobedience in dozens of southern cities to challenge segregated lunch counters and other public facilities. That spring they formed the Student Nonviolent Coordinating Committee (SNCC) to organize their sit-ins into a wider movement that swept the South. SNCC worked with the Reverend Martin Luther King, Jr.'s Southern Christian Leadership Conference (SCLC), which was a new organization composed primarily of African-American clergy dedicated to furthering the cause of civil rights.

By 1960, the 32-year-old Dr. King had emerged as the most influential leader of the nonviolent movement to end racial segregation. As campaign manager, Robert Kennedy tried to paper over the hypocrisy of the Democratic Party, which championed black civil rights in the North, while a wing of the party trampled those same rights in the South. The last thing Kennedy wanted was for racial issues to rear up in the last weeks of an election where the slightest misstep could determine the outcome.

On October 19, 1960, police arrested Martin Luther King, Jr., during a sit-in against segregated services in the Magnolia Room of Rich's Department Store in Atlanta. Newspapers across the country reported that a vindictive Georgia judge, Oscar Mitchell, used a minor traffic violation to refuse bail and sentenced King to four months of hard labor on a state road gang. King spent a harrowing night locked in the backseat of a police cruiser being transported across the Georgia countryside on the way to Reidsville State Penitentiary. It was the type of "night ride" that could easily result in a lynching for a southern black leader. His wife, Coretta Scott King, who was five months pregnant, was certain they were going to kill him. She called Harris Wofford, a friend of the King family and a member of the Kennedy campaign staff, seeking his assistance. Sargent Shriver, the candidate's brother-in-law, urged John Kennedy to call Mrs. King to express his concern, which he did.

Robert Kennedy wanted to avoid publicity that might remind northern black voters that the South remained a bastion of Democratic-led racial oppression, while at the same time sparking a backlash from southern white Democrats against the Yankee Catholic candidate. Shriver chose not to tell Robert Kennedy about the call. Lyndon Johnson had been working tirelessly to assuage the concerns of the southern wing of the party. When Robert Kennedy heard the news about his brother's phone call to Mrs. King, he scolded Wofford and Shriver: "Do you know that this election may be razor close and you have probably lost it for us?"

Yet within a matter of hours, while on a flight to New York, Robert Kennedy had a change of heart about the phone call. He became angered by the injustice of a judge sentencing King to four months in prison for having an improper license plate on his car just to punish him for leading a nonviolent sit-in. Kennedy decided to call Judge Mitchell himself. There are varying accounts of the phone call. Kennedy insisted he had nothing but a cordial talk with the judge. Other versions claim he denounced Mitchell's abuse of judicial power: "Are you an American? Do you know what it means to be an American? You get King out of jail!" In either case, Judge Mitchell decided to allow King to post bail. When the phone calls became public, Vice President Nixon had "no comment" on King's arrest, but he criticized Robert Kennedy for meddling in the case.

Whether or not it was Kennedy's intention, when the news spread of the two calls—one from John Kennedy to Coretta King, the other from Robert Kennedy to Judge Mitchell—the Kennedys earned the esteem of a large number of African Americans who deeply appreciated the gestures. The calls might not have been the determining factor in the judge's decision to grant King bail, but in the eyes of tens of thousands of black voters, it constituted national recognition, long overdue, of the injustices they faced. "I am deeply indebted to Senator Kennedy," King said, "who served as a great force in making my release possible. For him to be that courageous shows that he is really acting upon principle and not expediency." Black preachers throughout the country, including King's father and those associated with the SCLC, encouraged their constituents to vote for Kennedy.

Wofford and Shriver, who were the Kennedy campaign staffers most in tune with the African-American electorate, seized the opportunity of good will. They ran off over 2 million pamphlets on blue paper, which they called the "Blue Bomb"; it was entitled "NO COMMENT NIXON vs. A CANDIDATE WITH A HEART— SEN. KENNEDY: The Case Of Martin Luther King, Jr." The pamphlets contained quotations from Coretta and Martin King and from other civil rights leaders, praising Kennedy for his willingness to help Dr. King in his hour of need. On the Sunday before the election, they distributed the "Blue Bombs" outside of African-American churches, and the Kennedy literature flooded into black communities in crucial states.

On election night, Robert Kennedy set up a control center in one of the family's houses at Hyannis Port. There was a room with two dozen people manning phone lines, and the campaign's private pollster, Lou Harris, was upstairs in a small office crunching the latest numbers as they came in. The returns swung back and forth between the candidates all night long. Robert Kennedy "sat alone at the command post, his tie long ago discarded, shirt sleeves rolled up his forearms, waiting for something to break." It was not until 5:30 in the morning when the television networks named John Kennedy the winner. He edged out Nixon by only 112,000 votes out of 68 million cast. He won in the Electoral College 303 to 219, thanks to his showing in the densely populated and unionized industrial states of the Northeast and in Illinois as well as in six southern states that he carried with the help of Johnson. Voter turnout was 64.5 percent, which also probably helped Kennedy. The African-American vote had pushed Kennedy over the top in Illinois, Michigan, New Jersey, and Pennsylvania. There was evidence of voter fraud from both parties in several states, particularly in Illinois and Texas, but no formal complaints were litigated in the courts or sent to Congress.

After he had worked nonstop for 18 months to secure John Kennedy's victory, Robert Kennedy wanted to try something new outside of government or politics. But his father insisted that the President-elect name Robert to be his attorney general. "He is your blood brother," he told John. "Nobody has sacrificed more of his time and energy in your behalf than your brother Bobby, and I don't want to hear any further thing about it." The Ambassador's instincts told him that John Kennedy faced powerful enemies (some of them inherited from his father), and given his sometimes reckless private life and his hidden Addison's disease, he needed a loyalist in the attorney general's seat. Robert Kennedy did not want the job. "I had been chasing bad men for three years," he told William O. Douglas. "I didn't want to spend my life doing that." He let it be known that he would rather travel, practice law, become a university president, or perhaps prepare to run for the Massachusetts governor's office.

John Kennedy was the youngest President ever elected and the first Catholic. He had won a squeaker with no "coattails" to speak of, and he was attempting to initiate a "New Frontier" in Washington. Everything he did would come under intense scrutiny and criticism. Appointing his 35-year-old brother, who had never practiced law or tried a case in court, to head the Justice Department sparked cries of nepotism. *The New York Times*, which editorially lambasted Robert Kennedy his entire career, met the rumors that he might be named attorney general with scorn, arguing it created a bad precedent. *The Washington Post* and other influential newspapers criticized the appointment and voiced the opinion that Robert Kennedy was too much of a "crusader" who had neither the demeanor nor the legal experience for the post. Yale law professor Alexander Bickel wrote a lacerating piece in the *New Republic* in which he made the case against Robert Kennedy: "The sum of it all," he wrote, referring to Kennedy's work on the McClellan Committee, "is that Mr. Kennedy appears to find congenial the role of prosecutor, judge, and jury, all consolidated to his one efficient person."

John Kennedy knew his brother had no yearning for the job. He told Robert that others had made sacrifices to join his cabinet, including Robert McNamara, who gave up a lavish salary as president of Ford Motor Company to become secretary of defense, and

Dean Rusk, who resigned from heading the Rockefeller Foundation to become secretary of state. "You know, Bobby," John said, "there are people in my cabinet I don't know. They'll help, but they don't know my point of view. A relative is different. None of them can do for me what you can do for me. I need someone who, in difficult times, will tell me the absolute truth. . . . When things are tough and the administration is in trouble, I'll need you more than anyone else. . . . If I have the right to ask other cabinet members to make sacrifices, I can tell you I want you to be attorney general." John Kennedy refused to take no for an answer. Once again, Robert played the role of the dutiful younger brother (and obedient son) and capitulated.

On the morning of December 16, 1960, John and Robert Kennedy stood on the front porch of the President-elect's Georgetown home before an assemblage of reporters to make the announcement. Before heading out the door to meet the press, John said, "Comb your hair Bobby, you're going to be the next attorney general." And then he advised him: "Don't smile too much or they'll think we are happy about the appointment." Robert Kennedy would be the second-youngest attorney general in U.S. history, the youngest in over 140 years, and the first brother of a President ever to hold the position. In 1960, the Department of Justice had 31,000 employees and a budget of over $400 million. The attorney general's responsibilities included prosecuting federal crimes and representing the federal government in its civil litigation and Supreme Court cases, advising the President and cabinet on legal questions, managing an assortment of agencies as disparate as the Bureau of Prisons and the FBI, supervising all of the U.S. attorneys and federal marshals, assisting with the administration's legislative programs, and screening and evaluating federal judges. Robert Kennedy, who was 35 years old, became America's top cop.

"I thought Bobby could use some legal experience," John Kennedy jibed to reporters, trying to deflect their concerns. Robert Kennedy also attempted to blunt criticism with humor; he later told a lawyers group: "I started in the Department as a young lawyer in 1950. The salary was only $4000 a year, but I worked hard. [Pause.] I was ambitious. [Pause.] I studied. [Pause.] I applied myself. [Significant Pause.] And then my brother was elected President of the United States!" After a perfunctory Senate hearing, Robert Kennedy was confirmed by a vote of 99 to 1. He became the nation's 64th attorney general.

In the early 1960s, the Department of Justice faced a national crisis that stemmed from decades of festering racial injustice. Since the 1954 *Brown* ruling, state governments in the South had dragged their feet on enforcing orders to end segregation in public schools. Making matters worse, over a hundred members of Congress had signed the Southern Manifesto, promising to resist federal actions against segregation. The Eisenhower administration was slow to move on civil rights and took action only when there was a crisis, such as in Little Rock, Arkansas, in 1957, when President Eisenhower sent in the 101st Airborne Division to integrate Central High School. Eisenhower did not believe that laws alone "could change the hearts of men." As attorney general, Robert Kennedy inherited a federal court system clogged with lawsuits against segregation and a string of defiant southern governors, including Democrats Ross Barnett of Mississippi and John Patterson of Alabama.

Another crisis facing the Department of Justice involved organized crime, which operated from coast to coast on a far grander scale than had been previously understood. The extent of the problem was revealed in the tiny upstate New York town of Apalachin. On November 14, 1957, an alert state trooper happened upon a farmhouse surrounded by expensive cars, many of them with out-of-state license plates. State law enforcement authorities discovered it was a gathering of over one hundred of the nation's top organized crime figures from 15 states and from Cuba and Italy. Dozens of burly men wearing silk suits and gold chains dashed out of the building, and half of them were arrested. FBI Director J. Edgar Hoover had testified to Congress that he believed large criminal syndicates did not exist in America. Kennedy had been appalled to learn that Hoover had only 12 agents working on organized crime and over a thousand investigating political groups; he set out to reverse this ratio. "When I became attorney general," Kennedy said, "I proceeded on the basis that there was such a thing as organized crime . . . crime as a business." In 1962, Kennedy brought forth Joseph Valachi, a turncoat member of New York's Genovese crime family, to give detailed testimony about the inner workings of organized crime as part of a plea bargain. For the first time, Americans were exposed to the term *La Cosa Nostra*.

The Kennedy Justice Department sought to reinvigorate the Organized Crime Section, which was understaffed in light of the scope of the problem. Given that witnesses against the mafia often found themselves threatened or killed, prosecuting white-collar criminals was a daunting task. Kennedy appointed a tough young New York City prosecutor, Edwyn Silberling, to head the renamed Organized Crime and Racketeering Section. Silberling was experienced in prosecuting complex cases of loan sharking, extortion, gambling, prostitution, narcotics, and illicit interstate trade. Kennedy argued that "the racketeer is at his most dangerous not with a machine gun in his hands but with public officials in his pocket." Building on his work as the chief counsel of the McClellan Committee and his pursuit of Jimmy Hoffa (which continued), Kennedy and Silberling began ratcheting up the number of indictments of mafia figures. During his first two years as attorney general, the number of convictions rose from less than one hundred to over six hundred.

The "New Frontier" of the Kennedy administration sought to transform Washington from a dull, bureaucratic town to a center of energy and activity. The young President, the first one born in the twentieth century, and his 31-year-old First Lady, Jacqueline Kennedy, brought to Washington an élan of glossy optimism. They invited to the White House famous artists, musicians, and sports and entertainment figures. Most of the New Frontiersmen had served in World War II. They believed America could do anything if the people were united and determined. Arthur Schlesinger referred to Attorney General Robert Kennedy as the "nerve center of the New Frontier." Former FBI agent Walter Sheridan said of Robert Kennedy: "He inspired us. He was a zealot, and we loved his zeal. He turned a huge, slumbering, bureaucratic department into a vibrant, exciting, effective organization." A career lawyer who had served under Kennedy's predecessor as well as under Kennedy said that Kennedy had changed the department from "a Republican law factory with a staid hierarchy" to an action-oriented workplace. The Justice Department under Kennedy, a former aide later wrote, had a "sense of a mission, of slaying dragons, of fighting for a good cause." The crusade against lawbreakers fit in well with Kennedy's moralistic worldview, and once again he found his thoughts and actions in alignment.

Campaign reporter Theodore White said, "I wouldn't characterize Bobby as an intellectual. I'd characterize him as something more important: the guy who can use intellectuals." Kennedy named Byron "Whizzer" White, the Rhodes Scholar who had served in World War II as an intelligence officer, to be his top assistant attorney general. Joseph Dolan, a Colorado legislator, became White's deputy. The oldest person Kennedy appointed was 47-year-old Lee Lovinger, who would be in charge of the Antitrust Division. His youngest appointment was Ramsey Clark, whose father had been attorney general; Clark was 33. Nicholas Katzenbach, a former fighter pilot in World War II who spent two years in a prisoner of war (POW) camp (and an expert in international law), headed the Office of Legal Counsel. From academia, Kennedy named Harvard professor Archibald Cox to be solicitor general, and Harris Wofford became an assistant in the Civil Rights Division. Kennedy chose to pass up Wofford to head the Civil Rights Division because he was involved personally in the struggle. Instead, he named Burke Marshall, a corporate lawyer, because he wanted someone in that volatile post who was not open to attack for being too cozy with Dr. King's movement. He kept his executive secretary from the McClellan Committee, Angela Novello, and he appointed the Pulitzer Prize–winning journalist Edwin Guthman to take charge of the department's Public Information Office.

On February 10, 1961, Kennedy told his senior staff at their first meeting: "The government can't overestimate the effect of cleaning up its own house. That means in hiring, in elimination of segregated offices in the South, and a thorough integration of all its operations, South and North." Only 10 out of the 950 Justice Department lawyers were African Americans. The FBI had about a dozen black special agents out of a total of 6,000, including 2 who served as attendants in Director Hoover's office. Kennedy directed his staff to reach out to the National Association for the Advancement of Colored People (NAACP) and to the law schools to encourage African-American graduates to apply for jobs with the department. For the first time, blacks were appointed deputy U.S. marshals in dozens of American cities.

Kennedy had been settling into his new job, reorganizing the department and setting priorities, when a covert operation by the CIA, held over from the Eisenhower administration, transformed his role in the new government. In January 1959, Fidel Castro had led a revolution in Cuba, creating the first government in the Western Hemisphere to successfully oust a U.S.-backed regime. Castro was a lawyer from the Cuban middle class who had for years led a small band of guerrilla fighters in the Sierra Madre Mountains. By 1959, a social crisis on the island that had been brewing for decades exploded into a revolution of workers and peasants against the landowning oligarchy. The U.S.-backed dictator, General Fulgencio Batista, was overthrown after years of authoritarian misrule had eroded public confidence in his regime. In the beginning, the movement had the support of the educated middle class of Cuba.

President Eisenhower and the CIA believed that Castro's land reform program, involving the seizure of acreage from large landowners, smacked of "communism" and would set a bad example for the rest of Latin America. With popular support, Castro also shut down Havana's largest casinos and brothels, which had ties to American investors and organized crime syndicates. When the Eisenhower administration cut off economic aid to Cuba, Castro, who had not joined the Cuban Communist Party, began seizing the assets of major American oil corporations and other enterprises. In 1960, Eisenhower ordered an economic boycott of the island, severed diplomatic relations, and secretly authorized the CIA to begin planning a coup d'etat modeled on the CIA's 1954 overthrow of the democratically elected president of Guatemala, Jacobo Arbenz. As the United States tightened the screws on Cuba, Castro turned to Soviet Premier Nikita Khrushchev for assistance. During the 1960 presidential campaign, both Kennedy and Nixon promised to do more in the fight against Castro.

The CIA had briefed John Kennedy when he was a candidate about the 1,400 Cuban exiles it was secretly training in Guatemala and Nicaragua. The clandestine paramilitary force was ready to invade the island, which the CIA predicted would spark a popular uprising against the new regime. President Kennedy retained Eisenhower's architect of the plot, Director of Central Intelligence Allen Dulles, as a show of bipartisan continuity during the Cold War with the Soviet Union. Dulles was a staunch conservative who had little interest in Kennedy's "New Frontier." President Kennedy understood the CIA's plan to practice "plausible deniability" of any direct U.S. involvement in the invasion. The CIA painted several of its own planes with Cuban Air Force insignia, and the pilots pretended to be defectors from Castro's own military. They planned to provide air support for the invading operatives at the Bay of Pigs on Cuba's south coast. Less than three months after being sworn in, President Kennedy approved the assault, creating the conditions for the first major crisis of his presidency.

The Bay of Pigs invasion was a fiasco from the start. On April 15, 1961, Cuban military forces fired on two of the disguised CIA planes, which forced them to make an emergency landing in Miami. The Immigration and Naturalization Service (INS) in Florida told the press the pilots of the B-26 bombers were "defectors" and their identities had to be kept secret lest Castro's goons victimize their families. Kennedy's ambassador to the United Nations, Adlai Stevenson, told the world that the planes were from "Castro's own air force" that "took off from Castro's own air force fields." (They had taken off from Nicaragua.) Two days later about 1,400 CIA-backed troops landed in the marshy Bay of Pigs, and Castro's army and militias jammed them up before they could establish a beachhead. Cuban soldiers killed 114 of the invaders and promptly took 1,189 prisoners. About a hundred managed to escape by swimming to CIA boats offshore. The "popular uprising" against Castro that the CIA had promised President Kennedy never materialized. The Cuban people greeted the exiles not as "liberators" but as traitors working for a foreign government. The Pentagon and CIA pressed the President for air support to save the mission, but Kennedy refused.

Despite the efforts of a New York City public relations firm working for the CIA, which put out optimistic communiqués from something called the Cuban Revolutionary Council, the Kennedy administration's story quickly unraveled. President Kennedy turned to his younger brother to help him manage the crisis, appointing Robert to head a committee that included CIA Director Allen Dulles and General Maxwell Taylor (President Kennedy's top military adviser), among other senior officials, to analyze what went wrong with the operation. "It was Eisenhower's plan," Robert Kennedy said later. "Eisenhower's people all said it would succeed." And if President Kennedy "hadn't gone ahead with it, it would have showed that he had no courage." From the time of the Bay of Pigs invasion, Robert Kennedy was thrust very close to the center of decision making in the White House.

Robert Kennedy's subsequent report about the Bay of Pigs debacle emphasized several crucial lessons: (1) All of the leading figures in the Joint Chiefs of Staff and the CIA had "war gamed" the expedition, and they unanimously approved it, but its weaknesses were never debated beforehand; (2) despite President Kennedy's explicit order that there be no direct involvement of Americans in the operation, two of the commandos that first hit the beach in Cuba were Americans; and (3) there never was a plan shared with the President for the use of American jets in support of the invaders, and since the entire plan depended on an indigenous uprising that never happened,

U.S. bombing raids would not have changed the outcome. Robert Kennedy later told the press: "I can say unequivocally that President Kennedy never withdrew U.S. air cover. There never were plans made for U.S. air cover so that there was nothing to withdraw." Still the credibility of the new administration was badly damaged.

President Kennedy accepted full responsibility for the botched operation, which seemed to quell the public's concerns. His approval rating miraculously shot up. He fired Director Dulles and Richard Bissell, who headed the Clandestine Services Directorate of the CIA, which was responsible for the operation. Both of them had assured Kennedy that, even if the invasion failed to overthrow Castro, the exiles could go into the mountains and become guerrilla fighters. The Bay of Pigs taught John and Robert Kennedy not to trust everything the Joint Chiefs of Staff and the CIA told them about the world and to be wary of hard-line military advice. Investigative journalist David Talbot, in *Brothers: The Hidden History of the Kennedy Years*, shows that following the Bay of Pigs fiasco the Kennedys had a hostile relationship with the holdover leaders of the Joint Chiefs of Staff and the CIA.

The President elevated Robert Kennedy to a position on the National Security Council (NSC) that some aides called "number one and a half." From that point on, he helped manage all of the crises, both foreign and domestic, that faced the Kennedy White House. Robert Kennedy had become, just as Joseph Kennedy had predicted, the President's most trusted adviser and problem solver. A direct phone line was installed between the attorney general's office and the Oval Office, and the brothers spoke to each other five to ten times each day. "Every time they have a conference," Vice President Lyndon Johnson observed, "don't kid anybody about who is the top adviser. It's not McNamara, the Joint Chiefs of Staff, or anyone else like that. Bobby is first in, last out. Bobby is the boy he listens to."

Fidel Castro had become a grave concern of the Congress, the mainstream press, and Robert Kennedy. Kennedy got to work in the White House, convening meetings of his new NSC committee: the Special Group CI (Counterinsurgency). He demanded to see the internal documents from the military and the CIA prior to the operation and called for multiple briefings. He searched for new ways to overthrow the Castro regime, and he worked behind the scenes for the release of the Bay of Pigs prisoners by raising private funds and orchestrating cash payments to the Cuban government. He felt personally responsible for their plight, since his brother had approved the operation. Kennedy struck up friendships with some of the Bay of Pigs veterans, such as Roberto San Román, who he said could call him "ten times a day" if he had to. He believed in the anti-Castro cause. The scathing criticism of his brother for being "weak" on Cuba following the disaster stiffened his resolve to destroy Castro.

Kennedy pressed the CIA to come up with new plans for covert actions to overthrow the Cuban government. He saw the Bay of Pigs fiasco as a potentially permanent stain on his brother's presidency, and restoring President Kennedy's tarnished image was his primary mission. Kennedy was also known for his vengeful desire to "even the score" with Castro. He demanded that the members of his NSC committee come up with ideas about how to take down the regime, target Castro and his deputies, and prevent Communist ideology from spreading throughout the hemisphere. Most importantly, U.S. policy sought to constrain Cuba's ability to serve as an example of an alternative development model in Latin America.

The historian Robert Weisbrot shows in *Maximum Danger* that in the early 1960s anti-Castro paranoia ran rampant in the American political discourse. Capitol Hill was teeming with bipartisan opponents of the Communist regime in Cuba. By 1961, Castro had become the bête noir of the American establishment. The only group in the United States that defended him was Fair Play for Cuba, which was a minuscule far-left organization that the FBI had thoroughly infiltrated. Following the Bay of Pigs, the dominant criticism emanating from American elites was not that President Kennedy had made a mistake by invading Cuba but that the CIA and its small army of Cuban exiles had bungled the operation. Vocal members of Congress demanded renewed actions against the regime. The fiercely anti-Communist Cuban exile community in Miami was as loud as ever, and there was widespread support in the media for the United States to "liberate" the people of that "imprisoned island."

It was not until the 1970s that Americans first learned about several CIA assassination plots against Castro; some of them involving hiring mafia hit men. John and Robert Kennedy's role in these schemes became the subject of intense speculation. In his biography of Robert Kennedy published in 2000, Evan Thomas writes: "RFK's own views on assassination in the period have remained difficult to ascertain." Thomas notes that John Nolan, Kennedy's administrative assistant, "flatly denied that Kennedy ever ordered an assassination or even discussed the possibility." Robert Kennedy headed the administration's key Cuba committee, and according to Thomas, "there is little doubt that assassination plotting went on at lower levels of the intelligence and national security establishment." In the 1960s, there had been at least eight documented CIA attempts to kill Castro, including one plan by intelligence operative Desmond Fitzgerald to kill the Cuban dictator while he enjoyed his favorite pastime of skin diving. Thomas claims that none of these "harebrained ideas cooked up by covert operators" ever "got off the drawing board."

Discerning whether or not Robert Kennedy participated in plots to kill Castro is further complicated by the fact that the subsequent administrations of Lyndon Johnson and Richard Nixon were less than totally honest in acknowledging their own covert activities and tried to toss their dirty laundry onto the previous administration. For example, Americans learned in the 1970s that Nixon's secret operative, former CIA agent and White House "plumber" E. Howard Hunt, forged documents to create the false impression that President Kennedy had ordered the assassination of South Vietnamese Prime Minister Ngo Dinh Diem. The Kennedy brothers had learned from their father never to "write it down" when implementing potentially explosive (or illegal) actions. They were also dedicated practitioners of the doctrine of "plausible deniability." The spotty historical record suggests that the Kennedys might have heeded their father's advice and effectively covered their tracks regarding attempts to kill Castro, or their political opponents might have exaggerated the alleged plots, or perhaps it is a combination of the two. Robert Kennedy's devout Catholicism might have militated against murdering a foreign leader, but he considered Castro an "evil" influence in the world, and during the Cold War, anything was possible. Covert terrorism against Cuba continued during the Kennedy administration from CIA bases in Miami under the code name Operation Mongoose. But the Kennedy administration soon found itself with multiple crises on its hands.

On May 6, 1961, with the aftermath of the Bay of Pigs offensive still reverberating in the Kennedy White House, a racially integrated group of 13 "freedom riders" from the Congress of Racial Equality (CORE) left Washington, D.C., in a bus bound for New Orleans. The bus stations and bus lines throughout the South were segregated, and state and local authorities defied federal court orders to remove racial barriers. The freedom riders intended to travel through Alabama and

Mississippi to challenge segregation laws in public transportation. When they arrived at the stations, the blacks entered the "whites only" areas, and the whites sat in the "colored" sections.

In Congress, Democratic politicians from the South dominated key committees due to seniority and incumbency, and they could block President Kennedy's legislative agenda if they believed the Massachusetts liberal attacked their "states' rights." President Kennedy had already backed off a campaign promise to end racial discrimination in federal housing with "a stroke of a pen" by executive order. He had not been prepared for the level of congressional hostility to the move, and Kennedy's inaction led civil rights activists to launch a "pens for Jack" campaign. They sent to the White House thousands of pens and ink. Kennedy's critics demanded that he show "less profile, and more courage" on civil rights, playing on the title of his best-selling book. Kennedy's rhetoric about "bearing any burden" and "paying any price" in the defense of "liberty" did not always match his actions. But his words resonated with thousands of young people who were determined to confront segregation through nonviolent civil disobedience.

When the freedom riders stopped in Rock Hill, South Carolina, white vigilantes assaulted three of them, but local police quelled the fracas. In Winnsboro, South Carolina, two riders were arrested. When the bus stopped in Atlanta, they divided themselves onto two buses (one Greyhound the other Trailways) to make their way to Birmingham, Alabama, an infamous citadel of segregation. Six miles outside of Anniston, Alabama, a white gang from the Ku Klux Klan (KKK) brandished clubs and chains and attacked the Greyhound bus. They torched the vehicle with Molotov cocktails, injuring 12 people who narrowly escaped out an emergency exit. Another group of Klansmen assaulted the Trailways bus when it pulled into Birmingham. Informants had tipped off the FBI that the bus was going to be raided, but it was an exercise in futility. The FBI refused to protect the riders, and the local authorities' sympathies lay with the segregationist thugs. Theophilus Eugene "Bull" Connor, the Birmingham public safety commissioner, a committed white supremacist, looked the other way as Klansmen pummeled the riders. He told federal officials he could not protect them because it was Mother's Day and officers were in short supply.

The freedom riders had a constitutional right to travel between the states in racially integrated buses, and the federal government had the obligation to guarantee their safety if the local authorities could not or would not. Attorney General Kennedy sent federal marshals to Alabama and put together an ad hoc police force. The civil rights organizers, young and idealistic, with the Supreme Court on their side, were in the struggle for the long haul. If a few of them were arrested, they would recruit more riders to take their place.

"In order to insure that innocent people are not injured, maimed, or even killed," Attorney General Kennedy announced, "I would call upon all people who have a paramount interest in the future of our country to exercise restraint and judgment over their actions in the next few weeks or next few days." Kennedy then added a remark that drew derision from the activists. "What is needed," he said, "is a cooling off period." James Farmer, a veteran activist with CORE and a freedom rider who had been badly beaten, responded: "We've been cooling off for 350 years, and if we cool off anymore, we'll be in a deep freeze." When the bus companies refused service to the activists, Kennedy telephoned the head of the company, whom he called "Mr. Greyhound," and told him it was illegal to deny Americans the right to travel. He threatened the company with Justice Department action if it canceled its bus service to the South.

On May 12, 1961, 21 college students (18 blacks and 3 whites) boarded a new bus in Birmingham to finish the ride to New Orleans. When the bus stopped in Montgomery, despite prior warnings from the FBI that there would be violence, there were no police present. Instead, there were several hundred white hooligans armed with sticks, iron pipes, and guns. An angry mob followed two white women activists as they walked away from the station. A group of Alabama females singled the two of them out and began slapping them and hitting them with their purses. "You deserve what you get!" they shouted. "I hope they beat you up good!" An unmarked car pulled up to the curb, and the driver got out to help the women. Hate-filled young men kicked and beat him with an iron pipe until he was unconscious. It was Robert Kennedy's assistant attorney general John Seigenthaler, who was a newspaper editor from Tennessee and one of Kennedy's top aides in the South. He had a fractured skull and several cracked ribs. White ambulance drivers refused to pick him up. Kennedy called Seigenthaler in the hospital: "How's my popularity down there?" he asked. Seigenthaler wearily replied, "If you're planning on running for public office, don't do it in Alabama."

Recognizing that the local authorities were useless, Kennedy sent 400 marshals and federal deputies to Maxwell Air Force Base outside of Montgomery. The Justice Department obtained an injunction prohibiting the KKK and the National States' Rights Party from interfering with interstate travel. The violence in Montgomery became national news when the television networks belatedly sent reporters to cover it. Martin Luther King, Jr., flew to Montgomery (the site of the successful bus boycott in the mid-1950s), and stayed with his fellow pastor Ralph Abernathy. Kennedy was gravely concerned about the lack of local law enforcement in Alabama, and he sent in marshals using Border Patrol cars to cruise around bus and railroad terminals and to guard African-American churches. The federal presence was seen as an occupying force in Alabama, and it stirred the passions of the segregationists.

On Sunday evening, May 14, 1961, some of the freedom riders and about 1,500 sympathizers jammed into the First Baptist Church to hear Dr. King speak about the crisis. In the park across the street gathered what King called "an ugly mob" of several thousand white people who yelled epithets and threw rocks, bottles, and crude Molotov cocktails at the churchyard. As time passed, those in the segregationist gathering grew more unruly. They flipped over three cars belonging to church members and set them on fire. There were no local or state police in sight. Byron White, Kennedy's assistant who was in charge of organizing the federal response, pulled together about 50 marshals. The marshals formed a thin line between the church with its trapped inhabitants and the angry horde outside. They had nightsticks, tear gas, and sidearms at the ready. It was a tense and dangerous standoff. Back in Washington, Kennedy was receiving an education about the degree of southern resistance to racial integration.

During the confrontation, Kennedy made several telephone calls to Alabama Governor John Patterson, a Democrat who had supported John Kennedy's presidential bid. Patterson refused to speak to the attorney general. Inside the church, King, Abernathy, and others feared the mob might firebomb the building. The marshals had to fire tear gas to hold the crowd at bay. The gas wafted into the church's air vents. Kennedy finally got through to Patterson and demanded that he send in his National Guard to protect them. Kennedy wanted to pull back the federal marshals because he feared for their safety and their presence was adding to the tension rather than diminishing it. When Alabama guardsmen finally arrived, some of them waved Confederate flags, and they refused to allow King and his followers to leave their house of worship.

King telephoned Kennedy from inside the church and told him that Patterson's National Guard could not be trusted and that he should not pull back the marshals. A *Time* magazine reporter over-heard Kennedy's side of the conversation. King said the federal government had betrayed him. "Now Reverend," Kennedy replied in an even tone, "don't tell me that. You know just as well as I do that if it hadn't been for the United States marshals you'd be as dead as Kelsey's nuts right now!" (Kennedy used an old Boston Irish idiom that King had probably never heard.) There was a pause on the other end of the line, and King finally answered: "All right, all right." A few minutes later Governor Patterson called Kennedy and blamed him for sending the freedom riders into Alabama. "Now John," Kennedy said, "you can say that on television. You can tell that to the people of Alabama, John, but don't tell me that. Don't tell me that, John." By morning, the violent mob had finally thinned out. Kennedy, who stayed up all night in his office monitoring the crisis, was improvising new techniques in conflict mediation.

Throughout the spring and summer of 1961, over a hundred free-dom riders were arrested. Their courageous actions gave Kennedy a crash course in crisis management. Civil rights leaders demanded the Kennedy administration use the Interstate Commerce Commission (ICC) to desegregate all terminals and vehicles used in interstate bus and railroad service in the United States. Prodded by the gutsy actions of the freedom riders, the administration finally ordered the ICC to enforce the new laws, even in the Deep South.

By the end of John Kennedy's first year in office, he and Robert had learned important lessons about how to handle covert operations abroad and racial crises at home. But they also faced another challenge, one of a personal nature. On December 19, 1961, Joseph and Rose Kennedy were golfing at a country club near their winter home in Palm Beach, Florida, when Joseph suddenly fell ill and went home to bed. Nobody thought it was serious, and Rose continued with her game. Hours later it appeared that the Ambassador was in a coma. He had suffered a massive stroke. John and Robert flew to Florida on Air Force One to be with their parents. For many hours, doctors thought Kennedy would die. "Let him fight for his life," Robert told them. In the end, the 73-year-old Kennedy patriarch, once a vigorous businessman and diplomat, was severely paralyzed and confined to a wheelchair. He would never speak again and had to struggle just to utter a garbled "no" as his only word. John and Robert Kennedy had lost the guiding force of their young careers. It was Joseph Kennedy who had catapulted them to high office, and now he could no longer serve as their behind-the-scenes operator.

5

Attorney General

During the first meeting with his senior staff from the Justice Department, Robert Kennedy said: "I want to be informed. Do your homework. Don't let there be anything in your department that you don't know. Know every damn thing!" He sometimes interrupted briefings from aides to say: "Don't tell me what we can't do, tell me what we can do!" He wanted the attorney general's office to become more action oriented. Edwin Guthman recalled Kennedy's management style: "He demanded to be kept informed about everything that was occurring in the department, and accomplished this by keeping his door open, having frequent staff meetings and by getting detailed written reports each night from each division head." Kennedy's attorney general years confronted him with a series of crises and new challenges that would have lasting effects.

Kennedy prodded the Organized Crime and Racketeering Section to show tangible progress in prosecuting the nation's illegal syndicates. In April 1961, he demonstrated his commitment to the cause by deporting Carlos Marcellos, who was a mafia kingpin based in New Orleans. Marcellos had used fake citizenship papers from Guatemala to duck prosecution. He pretended to be a poor tomato salesman, but he was the millionaire head of a criminal organization that operated in several states. Kennedy ordered federal agents to snatch Marcellos off a New Orleans street, drive him to a nearby airfield, and fly him directly to Guatemala City. He was unceremoniously dumped at a small Guatemalan airport. It took Marcellos three months to return to the United States, where he faced INS prosecution for illegal entry. Although the case was later dropped, the harsh treatment of Marcellos sent a signal to other mobsters that the Justice Department under Robert Kennedy was serious about prosecuting organized crime.

In May 1961, Kennedy testified before the House Judiciary Committee in favor of new laws to fight the syndicates. His main target was interstate gambling because it functioned as the mafia's private banking service. Typically, the mob transferred ill-gotten cash from one state into the legal gambling system of a neighboring state, often horse or dog racing, thereby "laundering" the money of its tainted origins. Some of the profits generated were then used to bribe local law enforcement and gambling officials. In June, he testified before the Senate Judiciary Committee: "These hoodlums and racketeers who have become so rich and so powerful," he told the Senators, "if we could curtail their use of interstate communications and facilities, we could inflict a telling blow to their operations. We could cut them down to size." Kennedy's experience serving as the chief counsel of the McClellan Committee informed his anticrime work as attorney general.

The Kennedy Justice Department targeted racketeers by enforcing obscure sections of the penal code that made it a felony to lie on official documents. Suddenly, gangsters found themselves being prosecuted for false statements on home improvement loans, naturalization documents, license applications, Internal Revenue Service (IRS) tax documents, and Veterans Administration loans. The mafia specialized in setting up phony business fronts for its activities, which required falsified credit reports and other bogus documentation, so cracking down on this small part of a criminal enterprise had immediate effects.

By early 1963, the IRS reported that the revenue-producing features of the department's pursuit of organized criminals—fines, penalties, and confiscated property—meant that the program was becoming self-financing. The value of assets seized in the gambling prosecutions alone was over $700,000. In a single day, the IRS raided 158 locations in 20 states, and federal law enforcement officials arrested 127 people. Similar busts closed down huge outfits, including an upstate New York bookmaking racket valued at $14 million. The total value of stolen property and assets the government seized increased to a point where the Organized Crime and Racketeering Section of the Justice Department cost taxpayers nothing. It was among the most efficient operations of the federal government.

In September 1962, John and Robert Kennedy faced another crisis in race relations that, like the freedom rides, tested their commitment to civil rights. James Meredith, a 29-year-old African-American Air Force veteran, volunteered to become the first black person to enroll in the University of Mississippi in Oxford. Meredith was the eldest of ten children from a poor family in Kosciusko, Mississippi. In June 1961, the NAACP had filed a lawsuit on Meredith's behalf in federal district court, challenging the law barring his admission. The state of Mississippi appealed the case all the way to the Supreme Court, and after a year of legal wrangling, Justice Hugo Black ordered the University of Mississippi to admit Meredith. Mississippi's segregationist governor, Ross Barnett, vowed to defy the order, calling the federal courts "the evil and illegal forces of tyranny."

Governor Barnett had been elected by pandering to a fearful white electorate and by gaining the backing of the racist Citizens' Councils. Barnett, like other southern governors, claimed states had the sovereign right to "interpose" themselves between the federal government and the people. Interposition was a wild theory that dated back to 1832, when John C. Calhoun raised it in South Carolina. Robert Kennedy had no choice but to challenge the governor, who was a Democrat with powerful allies in the Senate, including Senator James O. Eastland of Mississippi, who chaired the Judiciary Committee. Eastland was in a position to block President Kennedy's judicial appointments.

Drawing on his experience with the freedom riders, Kennedy quickly dispatched U.S. marshals to Mississippi to protect Meredith. On September 30, 1962, at about 6:00 P.M., a plane carrying the new student landed at the Oxford airport, and then a car whisked him to Baxter Hall on the "Ole Miss" campus. Twenty-four federal agents formed a cordon outside Meredith's dorm room. A large crowd of segregationists taunted the marshals who stationed themselves outside the Lyceum, the administration building where Meredith would register for classes. They chanted: "Communists!" "Go Home, Nigger!" "Two-four-six-eight, we ain't gonna integrate!" and "We Hate Kennedy!"

Behind the scenes, Kennedy searched for a face-saving way for Governor Barnett to concede, thus avoiding a violent confrontation; he also stayed in contact with Senator Eastland. But Kennedy failed to recognize two problems: Governor Barnett's promises were completely untrustworthy, and enrolling the first black student at

Ole Miss attracted hooligans from throughout the South. Ku Klux Klansmen, leaders of the white Citizens' Councils, States' Rights Party activists, and segregationists of all stripes descended on the idyllic Oxford campus. By 7:30 P.M., a large and unruly white mob had overturned several cars, smashed windows, and begun throwing rocks and bottles at the marshals guarding the Lyceum.

The previous night, in the state capital, Governor Barnett stirred up his constituents during a halftime speech at a football game where the Mississippi Rebels fought for gridiron glory against the Kentucky Wildcats. To thunderous applause, he said: "I love Mississippi! I love her people, her customs! And I love and respect her heritage!" The exhilarated audience waved hundreds of Confederate flags and chanted: "Ask us what we say, it's to hell with Bobby K!" It looked like a white supremacist rally. Hearing about the spectacle, Robert Kennedy said: "I wouldn't have believed it could have happened in this country, but maybe now we can understand how Hitler took over Germany."

Back at the Lyceum, the crowd became even more belligerent. Deputy Attorney General Nicholas Katzenbach commanded about 160 marshals that surrounded the building. The mob chanted: "2-4-1-3, We Hate Kennedy!" and "Go to Cuba, Nigger Lovers!" The state law enforcement authorities were nowhere to be found, which meant that the lightly armed marshals, the focus of the mob's wrath, were the only ones left to maintain order.

Later that night federal officers fired tear gas to hold the violent throng at bay. At one point, enterprising hoodlums tied a brick to the gas pedal of a car and sent it careening into the line of marshals. Large pieces of concrete and hunks of wood fell from the sky and onto the heads of the federal guards, who were mostly wearing regular suits with armbands. As the night wore on, enraged young men began firing shotguns. Before it was over, 28 marshals had been wounded by gunfire, and 2 bystanders had been killed. Over a hundred marshals had been injured. "The eyes of the nation and of all the world are upon you, and upon all of us," President Kennedy said in a televised speech that evening, unaware of the escalating violence. "The honor of your university and state are in the balance." But the enraged crowd at Ole Miss was too preoccupied with pitching debris at the marshals to heed the President's words. While the riot raged, Robert Kennedy phoned Edwin Guthman, who was in Mississippi with Katzenbach: "How's it going down there?" he asked. "Pretty rough. It's like the Alamo," Guthman replied. "Well, you know what happened to those guys, don't you?" Kennedy was known to use gallows humor in the middle of a crisis to dissipate the tension.

Finally, at Robert Kennedy's request, President Kennedy sent several thousand federal troops to Oxford to restore order. Early the next morning the violence subsided, and Meredith, heavily guarded, walked up the steps of the Lyceum, the scene of so much trouble the night before, to solemnly register as the first African American at the University of Mississippi. Marshals continued to protect his every move. "James Meredith brought to a head and lent his name to another chapter in the mightiest struggle of our time," Robert Kennedy said. The NAACP field secretary in Mississippi, Medgar Evers, visited Meredith on the weekends to see how he was doing. It was important for the civil rights movement that he succeed. The following summer he graduated with a bachelor's degree in political science. The administration's post mortem of the Ole Miss disaster taught Robert Kennedy that he could not (even privately) trust the word of state officials that order would be maintained and that he had brought Meredith to the campus too hastily before security by federal marshals could be fully arranged. These were embarrassing missteps that cost two people their lives.

Kennedy could foresee the coming showdown with Alabama Governor George Wallace. During his 1962 election campaign, Wallace had promised to "stand in the schoolhouse door" to block the integration of the University of Alabama, the last bastion of segregation among universities in the South. "In the name of the greatest people that ever trod on this earth," Wallace exclaimed at his inaugural, "I draw the line in the dust and toss the gauntlet before the feet of tyranny. And I say: Segregation Now! Segregation Tomorrow! Segregation Forever!"

Kennedy understood the frustration African Americans felt with the slow pace of racial integration in the South. But at that time, he did not grasp the deeper critique of American society that underscored their struggle. Given Kennedy's limited experience with black people, he remained somewhat naïve about the discrimination they faced. Like most privileged Americans, Kennedy assumed that class and racial oppression could be readily overcome through determination and hard work. He sometimes compared the plight of blacks to that of Irish immigrants in Boston. "The Irish were not wanted there," he once told a largely African-American audience. "Now an Irish Catholic is President of the United States. There is no question about it. In the next forty years, a Negro can achieve the same position my brother has." This comparison rang hollow to some veteran civil rights activists. After all, they argued, the Irish did not come to America stacked like cordwood in the hulls of slave ships, torn from their ancestral lands and then sold as chattel on the auction block.

In 1962, Kennedy had a limited idea of the meaning of racism in America, but as with his other pursuits, he was willing to learn. He pushed the civil rights movement in the direction of voter registration, and to achieve that end, he formed the Voter Education Project (VEP). Kennedy wrested from Congress $5 million to start up the VEP. Southern white politicians were nonplussed; they knew the VEP was intended to help blacks assert their rights. For the first time since Reconstruction, the federal government buttressed the efforts of African Americans to register to vote in the South. Kennedy hoped to move the focus of the civil rights movement away from direct confrontations with the white power structure and toward winning the right to vote. With the franchise, blacks could elect a new breed of politicians more attuned to the post–Jim Crow era.

With regard to the issue of domestic Communism, Kennedy showed that, although he was a robust Cold Warrior, he was not an ideologue. He joked that most of the members of the tiny "Communist Party USA" were FBI agents who had infiltrated the organization. When Arlington Cemetery denied burial to a decorated war veteran because he had been a member of the Communist Party as a youth, Kennedy overruled those concerns: "If the people buried there don't object, why do those who are still living?" he asked. Another case involved an American Communist, Junius Scales, who was the only person imprisoned for violating the federal loyalty oath statute. Kennedy granted him clemency over the objections of FBI Director J. Edgar Hoover. And when octogenarian pacifist A. J. Muste of the Fellowship of Reconciliation (FOR) violated a federal ban against traveling to Cuba, INS officials recommended that Muste be picked up and his boat seized. After reading the document authorizing Muste's arrest, Kennedy threw it in the trash bin, "I'm not going to sign that piece of paper," he said.

However, Kennedy's magnanimity toward dissenters had its limits. When FBI Director J. Edgar Hoover insisted that a wiretap be placed on Martin Luther King, Jr.'s telephone, Kennedy at first resisted. Hoover claimed to have proof that Stanley Levison, who was one of King's top aides and a former member of the Communist Party, was using the civil rights movement as a Communist front. In February 1962, Kennedy signed the memo authorizing the taps on King and his colleague Levison. Approving the secret surveillance was an egregious violation of their civil liberties, and it made a mockery of Kennedy's rhetoric about sharing the goals of the African-American struggle.

J. Edgar Hoover had come to symbolize the past crime-fighting glories of the FBI, but he was a complicated figure who spent more time investigating alleged Communists than pursuing organized crime figures. Strengthening Hoover's hand were his thick dossiers filled with embarrassing and potentially career-ending information on many politicians, including President Kennedy. Hoover had evidence that John Kennedy, both as senator and as President, had been a prodigious philanderer. For years, Robert Kennedy had helped conceal his brother's infidelities. Given that Hoover possessed a devastating file on President Kennedy's sex life, Robert Kennedy was in no position to throw his weight around with the director. Hoover even had proof that President Kennedy at one time shared a mistress with a known mobster.

Hoover liked to remind colleagues that he had been head of the FBI a year before Robert Kennedy was born. He resented having to answer to the younger Kennedy, and his room to maneuver was circumscribed by the fact that his boss was the President's brother. Robert Kennedy's informal management style also irritated Hoover, such as when he brought Brumus, his enormous Newfoundland dog to the office or when he let his children run freely inside government buildings.

Robert Kennedy eventually arranged for Hoover to have a weekly private lunch with the President, and he tried to placate the mercurial director. Kennedy knew one of the reasons why Hoover asked him to sign off on the wiretap order was to implicate him on the record in something that could be damaging. Hoover needed no such permission to eavesdrop on King, which he had done before (and would continue to do throughout the Johnson and Nixon administrations, with the FBI's vast set of counterintelligence programs [COINTELPRO], against the civil rights and peace movements). During the Johnson administration, Hoover privately played tapes for King of him allegedly having sexual relations with a woman in a hotel room the FBI had bugged. Hoover's agents subsequently sent King an anonymous letter urging him to commit suicide or the tapes would be made public. There is no evidence that Hoover ever sought formal "authorization" from any senior official for these activities. Later he leaked to the press Kennedy's 1962 document approving the tap on King in an attempt to drive a wedge between Kennedy and his African-American constituency. When Kennedy was asked whether he believed Hoover was "a dangerous person, or just nasty," he replied, "No, I think he's dangerous." In another interview, he referred to Hoover as "rather a psycho." Kennedy's willingness to sign off on the wiretap of King was an expression of rank hypocrisy, but given the information Hoover possessed about his brother, he had little choice in the matter.

In the early 1960s, Robert Kennedy embraced a stylish new theory in fighting the Cold War called "counterinsurgency." "Counterinsurgency," he wrote, "is not a military problem; a military answer is the failure of counterinsurgency." He believed that "allegiance can be won only by positive programs: by land reform, by schools, by honest administration, by roads and clinics and labor unions and even-handed justice, and a share for all men in the decisions that shape their lives. Counterinsurgency might be best described as social reform under pressure." (Ironically, it was precisely these types of reforms that the loathed Castro regime was implementing in Cuba.) It also required U.S. military assistance to friendly governments to "put down Communist terrorism and insurgency." The Soviet Union assisted indigenous revolutionary movements in the emerging nations of Africa, Asia, and Latin America. To counter Soviet global objectives, President Kennedy created the Special Forces, the "Green Berets," which were designed to be as nimble and as brutal as their guerrilla enemies.

In the case of Castro, counterinsurgency meant arming paramilitary groups that harassed the Cuban government. Robert Kennedy worked with the anti-Communist Cuban exiles toward the goal of making life difficult for the Castro regime. Those who were willing to fight against Cuba were folded into a set of overlapping and illegal covert programs under the code name Operation Mongoose. With the help of the CIA, they formed small sabotage units based in Florida, purchased airplanes and boats, stockpiled armaments, and staged attacks. Observing these activities, Fidel Castro and Soviet Premier Nikita Khrushchev were convinced the United States planned to use the exiles in a second attempt to overthrow the Cuban government.

Adding to the East-West tensions, Khrushchev broke a self-imposed moratorium on nuclear weapons testing that had been in place since the final years of the Eisenhower administration. In October 1961, the Soviets detonated a monstrous 57-megaton hydrogen bomb. It was the biggest explosion in human history. The cloud of radioactive fallout thrice circled the earth. Kennedy's United Nations Ambassador, Adlai Stevenson, denounced the Soviet test before the General Assembly as a "somber development" that illustrated the belligerence of the Soviet Union and the global dangers of radioactive fallout. The United States immediately resumed its own nuclear tests underground.

The early 1960s brought a new era of nuclear brinkmanship. There were no treaties or formal agreements limiting the production, stockpiling, deployment, testing, or proliferation of nuclear armaments, and new delivery systems were coming on line on both sides. The Kennedy administration forged ahead with the Polaris submarine and approved the deployment of a thousand new Minuteman missiles, with the aim of maintaining the U.S. strategic nuclear advantage. American B-52 bombers of the Strategic Air Command were poised to rain hydrogen bombs on any Russian or Chinese city in a matter of minutes. The United States kept an eye on its adversaries through U-2 spy planes, which could fly at the unheard-of altitude of 70,000 feet.

In October 1962, U.S. reconnaissance aircraft photographed what appeared to be a half dozen missile sites, with more under construction, on the western part of the island of Cuba, near San Cristobal. Soviet military and civilian technicians were rapidly building the sites as if working under a deadline. The Soviet missiles in Cuba were unprecedented in the Western Hemisphere and could annihilate Washington in a matter of minutes. Khrushchev had dangerously altered the nuclear status quo.

On Tuesday morning, October 16, 1962, President Kennedy was briefed about the Soviet missiles in Cuba, and Robert was the first person he called: "We have some big trouble. I want you over here." They decided the best way to proceed was to keep the crisis quiet for the time being. To avoid suspicion from the press, President Kennedy stuck to his scheduled meetings and public appearances. He ordered his senior foreign policy advisers to arrive at the White House in as few vehicles as possible to trick reporters into believing nothing was amiss. Limousines pulled up with Robert Kennedy, Robert McNamara, and other top officials squeezed into the backseats, in some cases sitting on each other's laps.

President Kennedy then formed an "Executive Committee" of the National Security Council to pour over the intelligence and to formulate the American response. Called the "ExCom," the group included the highest-ranking officials from the Defense and State Departments, the CIA, and the Joint Chiefs of Staff. The ExCom met for the first time at 11:45 A.M. on October 16. It was the beginning of the most menacing nuclear standoff between the superpowers of the entire Cold War. President Kennedy chose not to attend all of the meetings, thereby freeing his advisers to express their opinions without the presence of the Chief Executive intimidating them or compelling them to tell him what they believed he wanted to hear. In the President's absence, Robert Kennedy's role was enhanced, though he listened more than he spoke. "Wherever he sat was one of the most important places in the room," National Security Adviser McGeorge Bundy said, "and everybody knew that."

At the first session, hard-liners from the military and the State Department called for preemptive air strikes without warning to destroy the missiles, followed by a full-scale invasion of the 800-mile-long island. Hearing the calls for war, Robert Kennedy slipped a handwritten note to the President's assistant, Theodore Sorensen: "I now know how Tojo felt when he was planning Pearl Harbor." President Kennedy held off the demands for aerial bombardment; he had to consider the possible strategic consequences of a U.S. attack on Cuba, such as a Soviet move on West Berlin. During the first sleepless night of the ExCom meetings, a tape recorder caught Robert Kennedy telling the group while his brother was out: "Assume that we go in and knock these sites out, uh, I don't know what's gonna stop them from saying, 'We're gonna build the sites six months from now.'"

The next day, Wednesday, October 17, U-2 planes discovered additional evidence of medium range ballistic missile sites. These missiles, which had a range of 2,200 miles, could reduce the response time to a nuclear attack on the eastern seaboard to two or three minutes. Still maintaining a veil of secrecy, President Kennedy kept to his original public schedule. He attended lunches with two foreign ministers and then flew to Connecticut to campaign for Abe Rubicoff, who was running for the Senate. He later feigned a cold and returned to the White House.

The ExCom deliberated over the next few days and nights. Robert Kennedy did not go home to Hickory Hill for six days. Unbeknownst to them all was the fact that the Soviets had already deployed more than 70 "tactical" nuclear weapons in Cuba. And Khrushchev had given great leeway to Russian commanders on the island to use one or more of the Hiroshima-size bombs in the event of a U.S. invasion. The possibility of the Russians detonating an atomic bomb over the heads of invading Marines was not a contingency given much thought by the members of ExCom. Indeed, it was not learned until decades later that the Soviets had a total of 162 nuclear weapons on the island and dozens of them had a yield 80 times greater than the bomb that flattened Hiroshima.

The hawks on the ExCom who called for a preemptive strike were overruled. Robert Kennedy believed it was vital to give Khrushchev a face-saving way out of the crisis. If a shooting war began between the two superpowers, he and his brother wanted it to take place far out at sea rather than 90 miles from Florida. Robert Kennedy led the group within the ExCom that favored a naval blockade. The faction that supported bombing forthwith included the Joint Chiefs of Staff (save one), former Secretary of State Dean Acheson, the CIA Director John McCone, Treasury Secretary Douglas Dillon, and President Kennedy's top military adviser, Maxwell Taylor. Robert Kennedy told Edwin Guthman: "It boils down to shoot now on the theory that the showdown is at hand and a blockade is only a time-consuming delay, or blockade and enter a very, very difficult winter and try to go the last mile to preserve the peace."

On Monday evening, October 22, President Kennedy revealed to the public for the first time the existence of the Soviet missiles in Cuba and announced that a U.S. naval "quarantine" of all ships going to Cuba would go into effect the following day. Ominously, the President declared that any discharge of a nuclear weapon in the Western Hemisphere emanating from Cuba would be considered an attack by the Soviet Union on the United States, thereby "requiring a full retaliatory response." (In the back of Kennedy's mind was Berlin, where the Soviets had the upper hand, and the possibility they would take the city as a strategic response to "losing" Cuba. This development could also lead to nuclear war.)

In the North Atlantic, the U.S. Navy established a 500-mile quarantine. No ship bound for Cuba was allowed to pass without being intercepted, boarded, and possibly seized. The Soviet Union denounced it as an "act of war" (which it was). The Soviet Navy sent a flotilla of 25 ships toward the U.S.-imposed barrier, along with a half dozen well-armed submarines. At the same time, American surveillance planes reported that the work on the missile sites in Cuba was greatly accelerating. President Kennedy ordered a higher level of military alert, and the Strategic Air Command put its nuclear-armed B-52s on a hair trigger. When Robert Kennedy was informed that top officials had access to a secret bunker in case of nuclear war, he said: "You can forget about that. I'm not going. I'll never go there. If it comes to that, there'll be 60 million Americans killed and as many Russians or more. I'll be at Hickory Hill." After an unforgettably tense morning, reconnaissance photographs revealed that the Soviet vessels had halted a few miles before the U.S. cordon. Some ships were lying at anchor, while others began steaming back.

The Soviet Union had "blinked" after going "eyeball to eyeball" with the United States, as Secretary of State Dean Rusk famously said, but the crisis was not over. There was still the problem of the missile sites that soon would become operational. President Kennedy sent Robert to seek out back channels with the Russians to discuss realistic ways to defuse the crisis. He met with Georgi Bolshakov, the editor of a glossy Soviet magazine in the United States with KGB ties. Bolshakov had been a frequent visitor to Hickory Hill, and he had a direct line of communication to the highest levels of the Soviet government. Secretly, Robert Kennedy used the U.S. military's Jupiter missiles in Turkey as bargaining chips, along with a pledge not to invade Cuba. Publicly, the Kennedy administration maintained that the removal of the missiles was unconditional and nonnegotiable. Robert Kennedy had played an indispensable role as his brother's special envoy.

When Edwin Guthman reminded Robert Kennedy that he was scheduled to speak before the American Jewish Congress in New York City on October 28, he replied: "That's one I hope I'm around to make." He understood the gamble that Khrushchev was taking: "They had nothing to lose," he said. "If we did nothing, we would be enfeebled in the eyes of the world. If we bombed, we would be the aggressors and they could do anything they wished. Or we could blockade and they could go before the United Nations and raise hell about us." The Joint Chiefs, and their hawkish allies on the ExCom, argued that bombing and occupying the island were the only ways to ensure the missiles were neutralized. The Russians, they argued, could not be trusted to remove the missiles themselves, even with United Nations oversight.

Eleven days into the crisis, the hard-liners on the ExCom still called for air strikes followed by a land invasion. The State Department set up a team to organize a post-Castro government in Cuba. Secretary of Defense Robert McNamara warned the ExCom that an offensive would result in "heavy casualties," including the deaths of possibly 8,000 Russians. President Kennedy did not like the military options. He pointed out: "After a bloody fight, they [the missiles] will be pointed at us. And we must further face the possibility that, when military hostilities first begin, those missiles will be fired." The Air Force could not guarantee all of the missiles would be destroyed.

On October 27, the White House finally received a letter from Premier Khrushchev. The letter was remarkable for its emotion and thoughtfulness. Khrushchev agreed to remove the missiles in exchange for a pledge from the United States not to invade Cuba. Hours later a second letter arrived from Moscow, this time from the Kremlin's Foreign Office. Its tone was harsh, and it demanded that the United States remove its Jupiter missiles from Turkey prior to any dismantling of Soviet missiles in Cuba. Robert Kennedy suggested the United States simply ignore the second letter and respond only to the first one. The original letter sounded more like Khrushchev's voice; the second letter hard-liners inside his government might have forced on him. President Kennedy chose to acknowledge only the first letter.

While the ExCom fashioned a response to the Khrushchev letters, antiaircraft fire shot down and killed Air Force Major Rudolf Anderson, Jr., while he flew a reconnaissance mission over Cuba. Major Anderson had been the pilot of the U-2 plane that had produced the original photographs of the missile sites. The Russians and Cubans had been warned that, if they blinded the United States by shooting down surveillance aircraft, it would make a U.S. attack on Cuba more likely. "The noose was tightening on all of us," Robert Kennedy wrote, "on Americans, on mankind."

On Sunday, October 28, between 9 and 10 A.M., a special bulletin flashed on every radio and television station in America, announcing that the Soviet Union had agreed to remove its missiles from Cuba. The crisis had reached its peak, and everyone was still alive. "Thank God for Bobby," President Kennedy said. Robert Kennedy's back-channel diplomacy and his cautious contributions to the debates within the ExCom were crucial to resolving the confrontation. (Robert Kennedy wrote a short book chronicling the crisis, *Thirteen Days*, which was posthumously published and subsequently made into a film and a television drama.)

Critics have pointed out that no "Cuban missile crisis" had existed until President Kennedy chose to forgo private diplomacy in favor of a public ultimatum and blockade. Others believe that U.S. threats against Cuba and the illegal sabotage operations that were run out of Miami provoked the Soviet Union to place missiles there in the first place. Arthur Schlesinger argues that Castro did not want Soviet missiles in Cuba and that Khrushchev was satisfying purely Soviet strategic objectives; therefore, Operation Mongoose and the possibility of another U.S. invasion were immaterial to Khrushchev's decision. In any case, the Cuban missile crisis stands as a historical test case of the prudent use of military force. Robert Kennedy later pointed out that 6 of the 12 top civilian and military officials had pressed for bombing raids. If one of those six had been President, he said, "The world would have been very likely plunged into a catastrophic war."

In the 1962 midterm elections, the Democrats fared better than most political observers had predicted. Typically, the party in power loses seats in Congress during the first midterm of a new administration, and John Kennedy's slender victory in 1960 heightened speculation that the Democrats would lose big. The Republicans blistered the administration for not doing enough to battle Castro and tarred the Democrats as "weak" when confronting Communism. With the peaceful denouement of the missile crisis and President Kennedy's firm public stand, his poll numbers shot up, and the Democrats lost only four seats in the House and gained four net seats in the Senate, including that of Senator Edward M. Kennedy of Massachusetts.

Also, as noted earlier, in 1962, Alabama elected by a large margin a new segregationist governor, George Wallace. During the campaign, Wallace vowed to "stand in the schoolhouse door" before he would allow any African-American student to enroll at his alma mater, the University of Alabama. Robert Kennedy scheduled a series of events in Montgomery, the state capital, to explain the federal government's enforcement of court orders in favor of integration. He reached out to the state's moderate business leaders, clergy, newspaper editors, labor unionists, educators, and lawyers.

In April 1963, Kennedy traveled to Montgomery. An angry mob dogged him wherever he went; one man held a sign that read: "Kosher Team Kennedy Kastro Khrushchev!" A contingent from the United Daughters of the Confederacy sat guarding an iron star that marked the spot where Jefferson Davis had taken the oath as the Confederate president. The mission of the matronly women was to prevent the attorney general's foot from treading on hallowed ground. Kennedy met briefly with Wallace in the governor's mansion. Edwin Guthman later wrote that after the meeting Kennedy had come closer to "throwing his hands up in despair" than at any other time. Wallace vowed to battle "the illegal usurpation of power by the Central Government."

In the spring of 1963, racial tensions heated up throughout the South. In Birmingham, Alabama, violent clashes erupted between the police, under the command of Eugene "Bull" Connor, and African-American citizens who peacefully marched to protest the city's segregated facilities. Martin Luther King, Jr., and the SCLC believed Birmingham the most fitting place to expose the nation (and Congress and the Kennedy administration) to the horrors of Jim Crow. When King defied a state court injunction against further demonstrations (a "pseudo" law he called it), Birmingham authorities arrested him and placed him in solitary confinement over the Easter weekend. On Sunday, April 15, Robert Kennedy intervened to secure better treatment for King. On April 16, King drafted "Letter from a Birmingham Jail" on the edges of a newspaper, using a pen smuggled in by a black trusty. It was a clarion call to his fellow preachers to wait no longer for social justice. "Freedom is never given voluntarily by the oppressor," he wrote. "[I]t must be demanded by the oppressed."

On April 20, King was released, and he joined the ongoing protests. On May 2, Birmingham police arrested over 900 schoolchildren while they peacefully demonstrated. King had urged the youngsters to join the marches in order to "fill the jails" of Birmingham. The following day Bull Connor's police force unleashed water hoses on the nonviolent marchers with the pressure set high enough to strip the bark off trees. Attack dogs tore at the flesh of dozens of children. Fifty officers randomly swung nightsticks into skulls. Television images graphically illustrated that the city of Birmingham, which tried to portray itself as a modern urban center, was in reality a racist backwater. A crude dynamite bomb exploded at the home King's brother, a Birmingham minister, and another one blew out part of a room in a motel where King stayed. Robert Kennedy persuaded the President to amass 3,000 federal troops at a nearby air base. President Kennedy also prepared to federalize the Alabama National Guard. After several tense days, the clashes subsided, and Birmingham merchants began removing racial designations from drinking fountains, restrooms, and lunch counters. The televised violence, just as King had intended, increased the pressure on the Kennedy administration and the Congress to take action on civil rights.

In June 1963, two courageous African-American young people stepped forward to become the first black students to enroll at the University of Alabama in Tuscaloosa. Vivian Malone, the 20-year-old daughter of a career military officer, and James Hood, also 20, planned to register for summer courses. Kennedy sought to avoid the kind of violence that had plagued the integration of Ole Miss. Governor Wallace vowed to block the students' admission and sent the Alabama National Guard to set up a command post at the tranquil, magnolia-lined campus. Kennedy sent Nicholas Katzenbach to Tuscaloosa to represent the federal government.

While they managed the crisis in Alabama, John and Robert Kennedy took the extraordinary step of allowing the documentary filmmaker Robert Drew to record the deliberations inside the Justice Department and the White House. Drew also had a team in Alabama that interviewed Wallace and filmed him planning logistics for the state troopers and the Alabama National Guard. The Kennedys and their top aides met several times in the Oval Office, where their candid discussions of the Wallace crisis were captured on film. They searched for ways to nationalize the Guard as quickly as possible if Wallace physically stopped the students from registering. President Kennedy, who was clearly worried, asked his younger brother if "pushing" the governor out of the doorway might be necessary. "A little pushing," he replied. In the film, John and Robert Kennedy complete each other's sentences in an extraordinary display of synergistic communication.

Robert Kennedy was the only cabinet member to advocate immediately sending a tough civil rights bill to Capitol Hill, which would be the strongest presidential stand for civil rights since Reconstruction. He also urged his brother, who looked surprised at the suggestion, to go on television and make a moral appeal to the nation in support of quick passage of the new laws. They girded themselves for the reaction of the southern wing of the

Democratic Party, which would do everything in its power to block the legislation.

On Tuesday morning, June 11, 1963, the film crew recorded Robert Kennedy having breakfast with Ethel and his children at Hickory Hill and then followed him to work. Inside the spacious, wood-paneled attorney general's office, the visiting filmmakers captured three of Kennedy's young children scurrying around. During one telephone conversation with Katzenbach, who was in Tuscaloosa preparing to confront Wallace that day, Kennedy briefly put his three-year-old daughter, Kerry, on the phone. Kennedy gave Katzenbach some last-minute advice about how to deal with Wallace, even suggesting the "tone of voice" he should use. "You can dismiss him as rather a second-rate figure," Kennedy said. "He's wasting your time, he's wasting the students' time, and he's causing a great fuss down there." "Good luck," he concluded. "You'll do well."

On live television, Katzenbach, with two marshals flanking him, marched at a fast clip to the steps of Foster Hall to speak to the governor, who was literally standing in front of the door to bar entry to the two black students. Wallace's contempt for the federal government was transparent as he cut off Katzenbach in midsentence, telling him not "to make a speech." Speaking into a bulky microphone draped around his neck, Governor Wallace bellowed that Katzenbach represented an "unwelcome, unwanted, unwarranted" intrusion on his state's sovereignty, which he said was a "frightful example of the tyranny of the central government." Robert Kennedy had chosen the right person to confront Wallace. The 6'4" Katzenbach had been hardened in a POW camp during World War II. He towered over the governor, and while television cameras whirred, he expressed his perplexity at the "show" Wallace was putting on. There was "no choice" for the federal government but to "enforce the orders of its courts," Katzenbach told him.

After Wallace defied Katzenbach, President Kennedy signed an executive order federalizing the Alabama National Guard. He stripped the Guard from the governor's command, and then Katzenbach successfully enrolled the students on the second attempt. As he left the campus, Wallace looked into the television cameras from the backseat of his car. "Next year there's gonna be an election," he drawled, "and whoever the South chooses is gonna be the next president. Cuz' you can't win without the South. And you're gonna see that the South is gonna be against some folks." Back in his

Washington office, a relieved Robert Kennedy lit up a cigar as news reports informed the nation that Wallace had backed down and there had been no violence.

That evening President Kennedy gave a televised address during which he announced he had sent a comprehensive civil rights package to Congress. "Where the rights of one man are denied, the rights of all men are threatened," he said. For the first time, Kennedy indicated that his administration was committed to passing a robust civil rights act. Later that night a Ku Klux Klansman shot and killed Medgar Evers, the head of the NAACP field office in Mississippi, outside his home in Jackson. It was the first of the high-profile assassinations of the 1960s. (Evers's assassin was convicted three decades later.) Robert Kennedy attended Evers's funeral, and he struck up a close friendship with Charles Evers, who took over the work his brother had begun.

Martin Luther King, Jr., and other civil rights leaders seized the opportunity to press Congress to pass the Kennedy civil rights bill expeditiously. What was needed, they determined, was a giant demonstration to demand passage of the legislation. The March on Washington for Freedom, Jobs, and Justice was born, and Robert Kennedy's Justice Department ensured that the expected 200,000 participants were protected from violence. Kennedy was intimately involved in planning the march, and he even reviewed beforehand the content of some of the speeches that would be delivered. The legendary founder of the Brotherhood of Sleeping Car Porters, A. Phillip Randolph, who had dedicated his life to furthering the cause of African-American civil rights, was the driving force behind the march. There had been other marches on Washington, beginning with Coxey's Army of destitute Civil War veterans in 1894, who demanded their promised pensions, and the aborted march in 1941 led by Randolph, which called for fair hiring practices for African Americans in the war production workforce. But on August 28, 1963, in front of the Lincoln Memorial, Martin Luther King, Jr., challenged the nation to live up to its promise in front of a gathering of a quarter of a million people. "I have a dream" entered the nation's political lexicon.

Two weeks later a bomb planted by segregationists exploded in the basement of the Sixteenth Street Baptist Church in Birmingham, Alabama. Four African-American girls, ages 11 to 14, were killed while they prepared to sing in the choir at Sunday services. King gave a stirring eulogy at the funeral, which became a civil rights rally.

Robert F. Kennedy with his brother President John F. Kennedy outside the Oval Office. Serving his brother's political career had been the defining element of Robert Kennedy's life up to November 22, 1963. *Photo Credit*: John F. Kennedy Library

Appalled by the viciousness of the attack, Robert Kennedy ordered the FBI to investigate the church bombing along with 28 other unsolved blasts throughout the South. The killing of Medgar Evers and the bombing of the church in Birmingham showed that any move by the Kennedy administration to further black rights would be met with escalating violence from radical segregationists.

There was still a long way to go in resolving the racial crisis, but with the Kennedy civil rights bill winding its way through Congress and the principal African-American groups focusing on registering voters and lobbying Congress after the March on Washington, there still was a cautious sense of optimism emanating from the participants in the "New Frontier." The last of the segregated universities in the Deep South had been integrated, and dozens of southern cities had removed their "whites only" signs.

In the wake of the Cuban missile crisis, President Kennedy signed the Limited Test Ban Treaty, which brought a slight reprieve from the nuclear tensions of the previous year. All nuclear testing now would be underground, sparing the earth the terrible effects of radioactive fallout, and a hotline was installed between the White House and the Kremlin to improve communication in the event of a future standoff. It was the first treaty ever signed in which the United States and the Soviet Union agreed to limit any aspect of the nuclear arms race.

African-American civil rights activists had precipitated crises that taught the Kennedys how to manage potentially explosive conflicts, and the brothers employed those same techniques to defuse the Cuban missile crisis. Confident in his record, President Kennedy looked forward to running for reelection in 1964. He hoped to win big, and he had ambitious plans for the future, not least of which was the technological feat of landing a human being on the moon before the close of the decade. The Kennedy administration had developed a systematic and self-confident manner of governance. "Everything was running so well," Robert Kennedy said.

6

Tragedy and Rebirth

On an ordinary Friday morning in November, Robert Kennedy attended a briefing with the staff of the Organized Crime Section. He learned that the number of indictments and convictions of racketeers was on the rise and that the new statutes for which he lobbied Congress were beginning to take effect. At lunchtime, he invited several aides, along with the visiting U.S. attorney in New York, Robert Morganthau, to Hickory Hill to continue the discussions over soup and sandwiches. Unimaginable events were about to propel Kennedy into a new stage of his public career.

The officials sat together in the backyard eating lunch near the swimming pool when painters who had been working on the house heard something come over their transistor radio. The workmen tentatively approached the group just before the telephone rang. At about 1:45, Kennedy received a call on the White House phone line. It was FBI Director J. Edgar Hoover. "I have news for you," Hoover coolly reported. "The President's been shot. I think it's serious." Kennedy clasped his hand over his mouth. He began trying to contact officials more knowledgeable about events in Texas when he received a second call, this time from Navy Captain Tazewell Shepard, one of President Kennedy's aides. His brother, Shepard told him, was dead. Two days earlier Robert Kennedy had celebrated his 38th birthday. His life would never be the same.

Television networks yanked their programs to cover the breaking news. Schools and colleges across the country sent their students home. Kennedy prepared to meet Air Force One when it arrived at Andrews Air Force Base and console his sister-in-law, Jacqueline, who had been sitting close to her husband in an open limousine the moment he was brutally slain.

While on a contemplative walk on the grounds of Hickory Hill, Kennedy told his friend Ed Guthman: "I thought they would get one of us. But Jack, after all he'd been through, never worried about it." The attorney general's office had received a letter about a week earlier from someone in Texas warning that the President would be killed if he came to Dallas, but it was not taken seriously.

When Kennedy began to think about who might be responsible for his brother's assassination, his first thoughts were aimed at the anti-Castro Cubans, many of whom were still livid at President Kennedy for refusing to provide air support for the Bay of Pigs invasion. After speaking at length that afternoon with Director of Central Intelligence John McCone, Kennedy phoned one of his own contacts among the Cuban exiles: "One of your guys did it," he said. Kennedy also suspected that organized crime might have played a role and that his aggressive pursuit of mob figures could have triggered it. His department had been preparing for another trial against Jimmy Hoffa, this time for jury tampering and fraud. After hearing the news that President Kennedy had been killed, Hoffa told a confidante: "Bobby Kennedy is just another lawyer now."

But this kind of speculation was secondary to the immediate tasks at hand. Kennedy met the newly widowed First Lady when she touched down in Washington with his brother's body. He helped Jacqueline plan the state funeral, which would include dignitaries from all over the world. President Kennedy would lie in state in the Capitol rotunda. Although obviously shattered, Robert Kennedy displayed strength for his family and for his six-year-old niece, Caroline, and his nephew, John Jr., whose third birthday sadly fell on the day of his father's funeral.

After the events of November 22, 1963, a lawyer from the attorney general's office recalled that Kennedy "was like a walking zombie in the Department of Justice from the day of the assassination to the day he left. . . . Looking at him was like looking right through him to the wall." Kennedy's professional duties were on hold while he tried to sort through the meaning of his brother's death. The latest tragedy brought back the feelings he had when Joe Jr. was killed in World War II and when his 28-year-old sister, Kathleen, died in a plane crash. He entered a period of paralyzing bereavement. He sought solace in poetry, in the classics, and in Catholic ritual.

He became fascinated with ancient Greek tragedies, existentialist philosopher Albert Camus, and a French poet named Gerard de Nerval, who was said to have walked with a lobster on a leash because the creature knew "the secrets of the deep."

In addition to his new role in the Kennedy family, he had to come to terms with the fact that Lyndon Baines Johnson, not his brother, was now the President of the United States. He found himself in a professional and personal wilderness. So much of his life's activity had been dedicated to his brother's political career. Making his grieving process all the more difficult was his abrupt subordination to President Johnson, with whom he had a terrible relationship. He no longer had a direct line of communication to the President. In a sense, Kennedy had become, as Jimmy Hoffa had said, "just another lawyer."

Adding to the awkwardness of his downgraded role in the Johnson administration, Kennedy inherited a wing of the Democratic Party that had identified keenly with his brother. Individuals and groups from around the country, the powerful and marginalized alike, gravitated toward him as John Kennedy's standard-bearer. Johnson, too, was thrust into a difficult new role. He promised the nation continuity, which included passing the Kennedy administration's civil rights bill and retaining most of President Kennedy's key advisers. He displayed sympathy to Jacqueline Kennedy during her painful adjustment. She quietly departed from the White House with her two young children and resettled in Georgetown. Tapes of telephone conversations between them reveal that LBJ had compassion for her loss as well as a tender relationship with the young First Lady.

Even so, there was no question that Johnson was the President now and things were going to be different in his White House. Robert Kennedy was appalled by how fast Johnson removed President Kennedy's belongings from the Oval Office to set up his own work space. Almost as a favor, Johnson sent Robert and Ethel on a semidiplomatic mission to the Far East. On the trip, young people enthusiastically greeted Kennedy at every stop, and he began to grasp President Kennedy's global impact. "He was not only President of one nation," Kennedy concluded. "He was president of young people around the world. If President Kennedy's life and death are to mean anything, we young people must work harder for a better life for all the people of the world." In the months following the assassination, Kennedy came to realize that millions of people who had looked to John Kennedy for leadership now looked to him.

Kennedy's supporters inside the Democratic Party called for President Johnson to ask him to be his running mate in 1964. National opinion polls indicated that three out of four Democrats wanted Kennedy to be Johnson's vice president. In March 1964, during the New Hampshire primary, a write-in movement started up to place Kennedy on the ticket. Over 25,000 voters wrote in Kennedy's name for vice president, which was only 3,700 fewer than listed Johnson's name for President. But Johnson had no intention of being overshadowed by another Kennedy, particularly young "Bobby," who he believed treated him disrespectfully. Kennedy coyly kept his name in the running, and Johnson pretended to be open to the move. Then, after leading Kennedy on, Johnson cut him off at the knees when he announced that he would not accept any cabinet member as his running mate and that Minnesota Senator Hubert Humphrey, whom Johnson could control, would be the vice president. Revealing his mean streak to a group of friendly journalists, Johnson, who was good at impersonations, mercilessly mocked Kennedy's sullen reaction when he was told the news.

On June 19, 1964, Senator Edward Kennedy was in a private plane that crashed near Southampton, Massachusetts, claiming the lives of the pilot and one of his Senate aides. The youngest Kennedy sibling had broken his back and was lucky to have survived the accident, which required surgery and months of recuperation. "How much more do they have to take?" Robert Kennedy asked Ed Guthman, referring to his mother and father. "I just don't see how I can do anything now. I think I should just get out of it all. Somebody up there doesn't like us."

After months of contemplating his fate, Kennedy slowly reentered public life. In New York, Republican Senator Kenneth Keating was up for reelection, and a large contingent of the state's Democrats implored Kennedy to challenge him. A seat in the U.S. Senate would give him an independent voice in national politics, free from the shackles of the Johnson administration.

At the 1964 Democratic National Convention in Atlantic City, New Jersey, the party's rank and file encouraged Kennedy to begin his own political career. Johnson feared that the assembled delegates, still grieving the death of President Kennedy, might be swept into an emotional stampede to put his brother on the ticket. Johnson conspired with J. Edgar Hoover to use the FBI to monitor the attorney general's political contacts during the convention. He also made sure that Kennedy did not address the gathering until well after Hubert Humphrey was safely installed as the party's vice presidential candidate.

Johnson's political instincts were probably correct. On the evening of August 27, 1964, when Kennedy stood at the podium to speak following a short film tribute to his brother, he could do nothing but gaze out at the audience while the delegates gave him a thunderous 22-minute standing ovation. He tried to interrupt several times to speak, but the deafening sound of cheers and applause filling the Atlantic City Convention Center drowned him out. Veteran political observers said they had never seen anything like it. The delegates' passionate response showed that the "Kennedy wing" of the party was still energized and looking to him for leadership.

Shortly after the convention, Kennedy announced his candidacy for the U.S. Senate in New York. On September 2, 1964, he resigned as attorney general. He had planned to be intimately involved in helping his brother win reelection in 1964, but instead he found himself seeking public office for the first time in his own right. Although the New York state Democratic delegation was excited about his candidacy, *The New York Times* and the *New York Herald Tribune* opposed Kennedy from the start. These two influential newspapers portrayed him as an opportunist and generally ignored the substance of his views. In what became a recurring theme, reporters for both papers zeroed in on the unruly crowds that swarmed around Kennedy at his campaign stops, implying these outpourings were simply the product of his celebrity and family name. *The Times* endorsed Senator Keating and hacked away at Kennedy with negative editorials. "Well, at least they can never say I got my job through *The New York Times*," Kennedy said.

Given that Kennedy had not lived in New York since he was a child, the Keating campaign labeled him a "carpetbagger." Keating, who was a two-term moderate Republican, offered to give him a map of New York so he could better get to know the state. Kennedy responded: "There may be some who believe that where a candidate voted in the past is more important than his capacity to serve the state. I cannot in fairness expect these people to vote for me, even though my mother and father had a home in New York since 1926 and I attended New York schools for six years." At other times in the campaign, Kennedy emphasized that he left New York only to go to college and to join the service. "I lived in New York for many years," he said. "But if this election is to be decided on the basis of who's lived in here the longest, perhaps we should elect the oldest man in the state." Polls showed that Kennedy's main vulnerability was the carpetbagger issue. Many New Yorkers believed he was using their state to further his own political ambitions. Kennedy pointed out to a friend: "It's funny when you think of it. Did you know they called my brother John a carpetbagger when he ran in Massachusetts? They said he should be running in New York."

Kennedy jabbed at Keating by playing on his ties to the head of the Republican ticket, the Arizona senator whose staunch conservatism alienated moderate New Yorkers. At a dinner in the Catskills, Kennedy said: "Senator Keating offered to send me a road map. Well, I don't need a roadmap to know how I feel about Barry Goldwater. I'm against Barry Goldwater. Barry Goldwater wants to give control of nuclear weapons to commanders in the field. Now that's my idea of high adventure. General Eisenhower says that he could live with a Goldwater Administration. Well, I suppose he'd have as good a chance as anyone else." Later in his speech, Kennedy said: "The Catskills were immortalized by Washington Irving. He wrote of a man who fell asleep and awoke in another era. The only other area that can boast such a man is Phoenix, Arizona." Kennedy relished the opportunity to contrast the Democratic Party with the GOP, and he utilized the skills he had acquired managing John Kennedy's campaigns. It turned out to be the only campaign in Robert Kennedy's life where he went head to head against a Republican.

During the campaign, in the bigger cities, Kennedy was known to fling open car doors unexpectedly and wade into the foot traffic. He walked the streets pressing the flesh and drawing crowds around him. Gerald Gardner, who wrote a whimsical book on Kennedy's bid for the Senate, physically described the candidate as "the diffident, shirt-sleeved fellow with the face of a worn teen-ager"; his "wounded smile on the bronze face suggested vulnerability, but there was a hint of steel in the mouth and jaw." Kennedy had a youthful, energetic persona, reminiscent of that of his brother, which politically served him well.

Although he had never run for public office, Robert Kennedy was an experienced campaign manager. He predicted to his senior staff: "I'll draw huge crowds as I go to different parts of the state for the first time. All the attention will be on that, and it will last for about three weeks. I'll hit a low point around the first of October. The question will be whether I can turn it around and regain the momentum." Kennedy also understood the tone the campaign must take: "It won't do for me to march into New York proclaiming the shocking, shameful state of affairs here," he said. "I'll have to take the position that New York is a great state, but it could be greater."

President Johnson and Vice President Humphrey came to the Empire State to help Kennedy. In October, Johnson attended several Kennedy campaign events, and he aided him in winning the support of New York City Mayor Robert Wagner. Humphrey told a White Plains audience: "There's a team that needs your support. It is the team of Johnson, Humphrey, and Kennedy!" Former President Harry Truman also endorsed Kennedy.

Democrats running for state office were often popular in New York City but faced deficits in the rural upstate regions. But Kennedy reversed this trend, putting in an impressive showing upstate, while there were significant defections among Democrats downstate. Among some New York City liberals, Kennedy's past work for Senator Joseph McCarthy and his prosecution of labor leaders had an alienating effect. The liberal ADA, which identified with the Adlai Stevenson wing of the party, withheld its endorsement. In the "Big Apple," Kennedy also had to contend with battles between turf-conscious party bosses, conflicts between ethnic groups, and politicians with their own personality cults. Some New York City pols ran their own fiefdoms and were players in decades-old rivalries that were nearly impossible to sort out. He avoided being sucked into these local conflicts.

Upstate New York was also contested territory because there were many Republican rural districts. At one stop, people with Goldwater signs confronted Kennedy and yelled: "Go back to where you came from!" Kennedy replied: "People have been telling me that all week, and that's why I'm here." In tiny Watertown, a little boy carried a large sign that read: "Don't use me in your cynical power grab!" Kennedy promised the child he would not. At Cornell University in Ithaca, Kennedy noticed a group of young people holding Goldwater signs. "I'm glad to see some people for Senator Goldwater here," he said. "It gives you the feeling that the two-party system isn't dead. I can't believe those people holding the signs are going to college."

When Kennedy stopped in Rochester, the scene of rioting in the African-American neighborhoods the previous summer, local Democrats told him not to broach the topic because they feared it would reopen fresh wounds. He ignored their advice. "In the South," he said, "you can pass legislation to permit a Negro to have an ice cream cone at Howard Johnson's, but you can't pass legislation to automatically give a Negro an education. I believe the community must provide education so there can be jobs. You have to give Negroes some hope."

Many black New Yorkers remembered Kennedy's role in helping James Meredith integrate the University of Mississippi and in standing up to George Wallace at the University of Alabama. When Kennedy campaigned in Harlem, a spirited crowd surrounded his car and prevented him from leaving. Kids let the air out of the tires, and he finally had to be whisked away in a police car. The campaign tapped into the enthusiasm the candidate generated in Harlem by organizing an aggressive voter registration drive as a follow-up to his visit. At times, Kennedy's Senate campaign had the energy of a grass-roots social movement.

In the final weeks, Kennedy leapt ahead in the polls, which provoked Keating to go on the offensive. Keating issued a barrage of press releases accusing Kennedy of running an arrogant and juvenile campaign and of being unfit to serve as a senator. Critics attacked Kennedy for staging events with his mother, Rose, and deflecting substantive discussion with charm and his family name. Keating dredged up a complicated legal case that had been settled when Kennedy was attorney general. He accused Kennedy of approving a deal that returned $60 million in seized assets to a German company that formerly had ties to the Nazis. In 1964, the horrors of World War II were fresh in people's memory, and Keating's aim was to play on ill feelings that had been directed against Joseph Kennedy for his soft stance on Hitler before the war. Keating was trying to drive a wedge between Kennedy and the Jewish voters of New York, which included many refugees and survivors of Nazi Germany. But the blatant nature of Keating's accusation seemed to backfire.

"In all my experience in political campaigning," Kennedy told the press, tapping his finger sharply on a table for emphasis, "I have never heard a charge as low as this one. I really expected more from Mr. Keating. I lost a brother and a brother-in-law to the Nazis. I'm not making any deals with Nazis." Kennedy's strident response prompted Keating to back off from his original assertion. Although

Keating dropped the subject, Kennedy told a few members of the press that it was still going "to have an adverse effect" on his candidacy. "People only remember the headline above the original story," he told a *Tribune* reporter, "not the denial. You never catch up with this sort of thing."

Kennedy met each one of Keating's smears with his own quick rebuttal. He scribbled one of his responses on a scrap of paper while sitting in a hotel room: "Kenneth Keating is conducting a campaign based on a most cynical exploitation of ethnic groups. First he accused me of making a 'deal' with Nazis. Then of being anti-Italian. Today he has charged that I sold out the Negro." He added: "These charges have two things in common. First, they are clearly intended to prejudice voters with claims that are transparently false. And second, they are issued by press release rather than before an audience of the people concerned—because my opponent knows they would be rejected by anyone who knows my record."

Late in the campaign and with great fanfare, Senator Keating challenged Kennedy to a debate and publicized that he had purchased a half-hour slot of prime-time television for the event. Kennedy concluded he had nothing to gain from it so he passed. Keating then tried to score a public relations coup by staging the "debate" by placing an empty chair in the studio with a "Kennedy" sign attached. All of Kennedy's aides were content to let Keating carry out his stunt without giving it added publicity, but Kennedy shocked them by saying: "I can't let him debate an empty chair. I'm going down there." He asked what time it was; 7:05 P.M. he was told. "I think I'd better get going," he said.

Kennedy, with a few of his aides and members of the press in tow, arrived at the CBS television studio where Keating was already on the air "debating" the empty chair. At the door of the studio, security guards blocked Kennedy's entrance. "They have just announced on the air that I am not here," Kennedy protested. "This is unfair and I insist on being admitted." He was improvising—and not in the least worried about how journalists perceived his impromptu appearance. When the program ended, members of the New York press flung open the studio doors and stormed in to ask Keating why he forced Kennedy to wait outside. But Keating and his aides scurried out of the building as fast as they could, hurling furniture and potted plants in the path of the oncoming reporters to avoid answering questions.

The nondebate came in the closing days, and Kennedy played it to the hilt: "Senator Keating really kicked that empty chair all over the studio," he sarcastically told crowds at campaign stops. "No question about it. He beat that chair. And there I was, outside the studio door with three of his guards." Not to be outdone, Keating purchased more television time and again demanded that Kennedy debate him. Kennedy flatly refused: "My schedule is set," he said. He was not going to allow Keating to gain the upper hand. At one campaign event, Kennedy told the crowd that he couldn't understand why Keating wished to debate him when "he did so well against an empty chair." A veteran chronicler of New York politics said of Kennedy's spontaneous trip to the studio: "What a combination of luck and guts!"

In the end, Kennedy beat Keating 3,823,749 votes to 3,104,056. Johnson's crushing victory over Goldwater in the state helped Kennedy. In his victory speech at the Statler Hilton Hotel in Manhattan, Kennedy said: "I believe this vote is a mandate to continue the efforts began by my brother four years ago—the effort to get something started in this country—and a vote of confidence for Lyndon Johnson and Hubert Humphrey." Keating gave his concession speech with Senator Jacob Javits and Governor Nelson Rockefeller somberly staring over his shoulders. Kennedy celebrated his victory at Delmonico's, near Park Avenue, with a glittery group of supporters that included some famous entertainers.

On January 5, 1965, Kennedy began his term as the junior senator from New York. He became part of the 89th Congress and part of the Democrats' 36-seat majority in the Senate. His prior experiences had been far different from the clubby atmosphere of the Senate, and he had to adjust to being one voice in a hundred. Kennedy's status as the brother and confidante of the late President set him apart. When he gave speeches on the Senate floor, the press gallery was usually full, and dozens of senators frequently attended. His first speech was on nuclear proliferation, and it drew about 50 senators as spectators. When a committee chairman heard complaints that Kennedy received preferential treatment for a freshman, he replied: "Oh, no, I treat him the same way I'd treat any future President."

When he joined the Senate, Kennedy recruited people who had served his brother as well as others from the Justice Department and the McClellan Committee staff. He brought on two young aides, legislative assistant Peter Edelman, who was 30 years old, and speechwriter Adam Walinsky, who was 29. He maintained a balance among his advisers between what might be called the pragmatists and the idealists. The cooler, more conventional counsel of Arthur Schlesinger, Jr., and Theodore Sorensen, both former advisers to President Kennedy, offset the younger firebrands on his staff. And when the situation required hard-nosed political advice, Kennedy turned to two professional politicians: Frederick Dutton, a Washington lawyer, campaign manager, and former adviser to President Kennedy; and Joseph Dolan, a skilled political operative and former Colorado state legislator. Kennedy tapped Frank Mankiewicz, who had been the director of the Peace Corps, to be his press secretary, and he also appointed Richard Goodwin to be a speechwriter.

He settled into his new job with the help of his brother, Massachusetts Senator Edward Kennedy, whose demeanor seemed well suited for the Senate. But Robert Kennedy had little time before he faced his first public rift with the Johnson administration. On April 14, 1965, President Johnson sent 23,000 U.S. Marines into the Dominican Republic to crush what he considered to be an anti-U.S. revolution on the island. Foreign capitals, especially in Latin America, viewed the intervention as an example of old-style Yankee imperialism.

In May 1965, in a speech on the Senate floor, Kennedy called the invasion a "tragic event" that made a mockery of the founding principles of the Organization of American States (OAS). The OAS, a Latin American alliance that had been established during the Truman administration, strictly forbade violations of the sovereignty of member states. (Kennedy chose to forget about the Kennedy administration's Bay of Pigs invasion of Cuba, which was also a breach of the OAS charter.) He said that Johnson's Dominican intervention trampled the autonomy of a neighboring state and imperiled "the structure of [international] law in the hemisphere." He also called it a severe blow to President Kennedy's system of diplomatic and economic initiatives in Latin America, known as the Alliance for Progress. "Our objective," he said, "must surely be not to drive the genuine democrats in the Dominican revolution into association with the Communists by blanket characterizations and condemnation of their revolution."

Kennedy's harsh criticism of Johnson's use of military force in the Dominican Republic less than four months after he joined the Senate showed that his thinking on U.S.–Latin American relations had matured. It also revealed that he intended to use his new-found independence as the junior senator from New York to stake out positions for himself that were starkly at odds with those of the Johnson administration.

Johnson claimed that the U.S. military action was necessary to prevent another Cuba in the hemisphere and that he was surprised to hear Kennedy, who had been a zealous foe of Castro and who had plotted his overthrow and possibly his assassination, condemn the attack. Public opinion was not on Kennedy's side. A Gallup poll found that more than three-quarters of the American people approved of Johnson's handling of the Dominican Republic.

Overlooked by the press at the time, in the same speech Kennedy linked the Dominican invasion to Johnson's military tactics in Vietnam. The Johnson administration policies in the Caribbean and Southeast Asia, he said, were part of a "seamless web," which relied too heavily on brute force. Kennedy's early critique of Johnson's tactics revealed, albeit indirectly, his misgivings about seeking military solutions. Although Kennedy said that withdrawing the 25,000 or so U.S. military "advisers" from Vietnam would be "an explicit and gross betrayal" of those "who have been encouraged by our support to oppose the spread of communism," he added, "the course of purposely enlarging the war would be a deep and terrible decision." Kennedy sought a "third course" for the United States in Vietnam that emphasized negotiations. "I do not believe we should be under the self-delusion that this military effort will bring Ho Chi Minh or the Vietcong to their knees," he said.

Kennedy was in a delicate position when he criticized Johnson's Southeast Asia policy because his brother's administration had been instrumental in expanding the American military presence there. President Kennedy had increased the number of U.S. military "advisers" from about 600 to over 16,000, and he approved the bombing and defoliation of parts of South Vietnam where the insurgency was strongest. Vietnam was also the site of the Kennedy administration's experiments with counterinsurgency, as "strategic hamlets" were constructed to corral large numbers of civilians into fortified zones where the Saigon government had greater control. As an active member of the National Security Council, Robert Kennedy had supported most of these moves. In 1962, Kennedy had told an audience in Saigon: "We're going to win." In the view of Johnson's allies, Kennedy was in no position to disparage the escalation of the conflict because his brother worsened the situation in

Vietnam, most of all, by overthrowing the government of Prime Minister Ngo Dinh Diem.

Back in the mid-1950s, President Eisenhower had used the CIA to install Ngo Dinh Diem as the leader of the "Republic of Vietnam" (South Vietnam). Diem came from the Catholic ruling elite. His brother, Ngo Dinh Nhu, ran a CIA-trained secret police that terrorized opponents. In January 1961, when President Kennedy took office, South Vietnam was already in crisis. Eisenhower's military "advisers" secretly fought combat missions, and the political repression of Nhu's security forces alienated the peasantry. Diem cut out the Buddhist organizations from a share of power in a nation that was 80 percent Buddhist, and he favored his allies and kin from the Catholic mandarin class. President Kennedy accepted Eisenhower's argument that Diem was crucial for containing the spread of Communism in Asia.

Throughout his first two years in office, President Kennedy propped up Diem with large infusions of American economic and military aid. In the spring of 1963, when Diem and Nhu cracked down on their opponents in the Buddhist centers in Hue and other cities, killing monks and burning down pagodas, they sparked a backlash from the Buddhist majority. Thousands of protesters descended on Saigon, clogging the streets of the capital with ongoing anti-Diem demonstrations. Kennedy's top advisers concluded that, as long as the Buddhists controlled the streets, the U.S.-backed Army of the Republic of Vietnam (ARVN) could not effectively fight the Communists, who were backed by the nationalistic government of Ho Chi Minh in Hanoi.

Amidst the huge protests, a Buddhist spiritual leader, Thich Quang Duc, engaged in a traditional form of protest that horrified the West: He immolated himself on a Saigon street corner. Photographs of the robed monk engulfed in flames, with witnesses praying nearby, were on the front pages of every major newspaper. Madam Nhu, the flamboyant wife of Ngo Dinh Nhu and Diem's sister-in-law, callously called it a "Buddhist barbecue." Other Buddhist monks committed suicide via self-immolation on August 5, 15, and 18. The South Vietnamese government's repression and the loss of control of Saigon led Kennedy's National Security Council to seek alternatives to Diem.

Kennedy's NSC was divided into two camps on whether to oust Diem. Both groups agreed that the war against the guerrillas had to be waged more forcefully, but they differed on whether Diem was the right man for the job. Robert Kennedy had been a member of the more cautious group, which advocated staying with Diem not because he was the ideal leader but because replacing him could create more difficulties than it solved. According to biographer Evan Thomas, Kennedy said on October 25, 1963: "If it comes off and it's not effective, then obviously the United States is going to be blamed for it, particularly if some of these people are caught and they talk about the conversations they had with the United States." Four days later Robert Kennedy "came out flatly against a coup." He feared that his brother might have another Bay of Pigs on his hands.

The White House tape-recording system captured Robert Kennedy saying on October 29: "I may be in the minority. I just don't see that this makes any sense, on the face of it. We're putting the whole future of the country—and really, Southeast Asia—in the hands of somebody we don't know very well." If the coup failed, Kennedy cautioned, "they're gonna say the United States was behind it. I would think that we're just going down the road to disaster." President Kennedy, apparently persuaded by those in the NSC who favored ousting Diem, approved the coup, knowing that General Paul Harkins, who was the U.S. military commander in South Vietnam, opposed the move for the same reasons as Robert Kennedy.

The plan was for the United States to signal Diem's chosen successor, General Duong Van Minh, with a "green light" by shutting off aid to the Saigon government. However, the plotting generals in Saigon, fearing a double cross, refused to reveal the exact day and time of the coup. On the night of November 1, 1963, General Minh's soldiers moved on the presidential palace and imposed a curfew. Diem and Nhu fled. They had successfully thwarted coup attempts in the past, and they believed they could rally their allies inside the ARVN to organize a "countercoup" against the generals.

The next day soldiers under the command of the new junta located and arrested Diem and Nhu, tied them up in the back of a Land Rover, and riddled their bodies with bullets. It was an ignominious end for a leader that the United States had supported for eight years and that Lyndon Johnson had once called the "Churchill of Asia." President Kennedy was speechless when he heard the news of the killings. Kennedy did not intend for Diem to be executed; he thought the millionaire prime minister would retire peacefully in Hawaii. The American people were kept in the dark about the extent of U.S. involvement. The Kennedy administration held to the story that it was an "internal" Vietnamese matter that had caught the United States by surprise. The episode marked a low point for John F. Kennedy's "New Frontier" and created, as Robert Kennedy had feared, an even more combustible political environment in Saigon.

In 1965, when Senator Kennedy began criticizing Johnson's Vietnam policies, his credibility was questioned not only because of the past actions of his brother but also because of the fact that Johnson had retained most of President Kennedy's key foreign policy advisers. Secretary of State Dean Rusk, Secretary of Defense Robert McNamara, and National Security Adviser McGeorge Bundy were holdovers from the Kennedy administration, and they became central figures in formulating Johnson's Vietnam policies. Johnson's allies never tired of emphasizing that their Vietnam policy was consistent with that of the previous administration so, if Robert Kennedy criticized Johnson, it would be like criticizing his own brother. Robert Kennedy never accepted this argument.

In March 1965, Johnson sent 3,500 Marines to Vietnam to guard the U.S. air base at Danang, which had come under attack as one of the points of departure for a bombing campaign called "Rolling Thunder," which targeted the Democratic Republic of Vietnam (North Vietnam). Johnson escalated the American military presence in South Vietnam to support the shaky new government of General Nguyen Khanh, who had come to power in yet another U.S.-backed coup the previous year. He refused to negotiate with the government in Hanoi unless its leader, Ho Chi Minh, accepted the permanent partition of Vietnam at the 17th parallel. Johnson, unlike President Kennedy, decided to "internationalize" the conflict by bombing North Vietnam and to "Americanize" it by sending in the Marines.

During his first 14 months in the Senate, Robert Kennedy's views on Vietnam shifted steadily from tactical critiques to a more fundamental questioning of the United States' ultimate goals in Southeast Asia, especially as they related to Johnson's repeated calls for "unconditional negotiations." He denounced Johnson's bombing of North Vietnam, and he questioned the wisdom of increasing the number of American combat troops. He also spoke out against the President's dismissive attitude toward the most important enemy faction operating in South Vietnam, the National Liberation Front (NLF). The NLF had been formed in 1960 to lead a guerrilla war against the U.S.-backed government.

It was an umbrella organization that represented Vietnamese nationalist groups of a variety of ideological stripes. Kennedy tried to show that, despite the administration's claims of seeking "peace" in Vietnam, its military and diplomatic actions precluded any hope for a negotiated settlement.

In July 1965, when Johnson decided to take the final plunge into the frigid waters of a massive commitment of U.S. ground forces in Vietnam, Kennedy called for a negotiated settlement and stressed that there could be no progress without social and political reforms. He emphasized the class injustices and vestiges of French colonialism in Vietnamese society, saying that the inequality of land ownership impeded the American objective of winning popular support for the Saigon government. Rare among mainstream politicians at the time, Kennedy recognized that the NLF, which the Americans called the "Vietcong," was the key political entity fighting the United States and it could not be brushed off.

In 1965 and 1966, questioning the Johnson administration's policies in Southeast Asia was a perilous path for any senator. The President's hard line had the solid backing of a formidable coalition. In addition to powerful members of Congress, such as the chairman of the Senate Armed Services Committee, Henry "Scoop" Jackson of Washington, and Speaker of the House John McCormack, Johnson had the support of World War II heroes such as General Omar Bradley and of former Presidents Harry Truman and Dwight Eisenhower. Prominent Republicans, such as North Dakota Senator Karl Mundt, a member of the Foreign Relations Committee, and the House minority leader, Gerald Ford of Michigan, were vocal supporters of the war. Republican criticisms of Johnson centered on the claim that he had not sufficiently unleashed the U.S. military in Vietnam. Johnson could also count on many influential pro-war media commentators, including Joseph Alsop, Drew Pearson, Robert Novak, Rowland Evans, and dozens of less famous pundits.

A Harris poll taken at the time of Kennedy's Dominican Republic speech in May 1965 showed that 57 percent of Americans approved of Johnson's escalation of troops in Vietnam. Throughout 1965 and 1966, whenever Johnson bombed North Vietnam, his popularity increased, illustrating the nation's martial spirit in the epic struggle against Asian Communism. Containing the Soviet Union and "Red" China by Americanizing the war in Vietnam was seen as a prudent and popular course.

Kennedy's biggest flap of his first year in the Senate occurred at an informal press conference at the University of Southern California (USC). In November 1965, he visited the USC campus, where college students peppered him with questions about where he stood on the war. He defended the rights of citizens to protest and even resist the draft if they were willing to accept the consequences. He hoped for a negotiated settlement but stopped short of calling for a U.S. withdrawal. A student reporter then queried him about a related issue:

PRESS: What about giving blood to the North Vietnamese?

KENNEDY: I think that would be a good idea.

PRESS: Is that going too far?

KENNEDY: If we've given all the blood that is needed to the South Vietnamese. I'm in favor of giving anybody who needs blood, I'm in favor of them having blood.

PRESS: Even to the North Vietnamese?

KENNEDY: Yes.

PRESS: Senator, there's one view that a lot of this difficulty was touched off by a lack of . . .

KENNEDY [INTERRUPTING]: I'd rather concentrate on the South Vietnamese and those who need it, but I'm in favor of giving blood to anyone who needs it.

Editorialists and political commentators pounced on Kennedy's apparent endorsement of sending blood to people who were killing American soldiers. Soon the right-wing John Birch Society set up a telephone line in Washington, D.C., where a taped message asked callers: "Isn't advocating the giving of blood to the enemy treason?" Alabama Governor George Wallace referred to Kennedy at a press conference simply as that "fellow who advocated giving blood to the Vietcong." The episode dogged Kennedy for years, and his office sent out disclaimers to angry constituents clarifying that he advocated giving blood only to innocent civilians.

On December 24, 1965, Johnson put into effect a pause in the bombing of North Vietnam, but after 37 days, he ordered the B-52s back on the offensive. The President used what the press dubbed his "peace offensive" to show that the United States was willing to go the extra mile before launching the next phase of the military buildup. He knew Hanoi would reject the offer to begin talks because Ho Chi Minh firmly declared there could be no negotiations until the United States unconditionally stopped the bombing.

Johnson then approved Operation Masher in South Vietnam, which *The New York Times* described as "the largest amphibious operation by United States Marines since the 1950 Inchon landing in Korea."

Robert Kennedy found Johnson's decisions regrettable. "Obviously the resumption of bombing in the North is not a policy, and we should not delude ourselves that it offers a painless method of winning the war. For if we regard bombing as the answer in Vietnam, we are headed straight for disaster." Kennedy again emphasized the social inequality inside South Vietnam: "We are spending far more on military efforts than on all the education, land reform, and welfare programs which might convince a young South Vietnamese that his future is not best served by the Communists."

On Saturday morning, February 19, 1966, Kennedy held a brief press conference in his Senate office, during which he raised the issue of the political role of the NLF. His latest statement, like his other public comments critical of the administration, exhibited a high degree of caution and avoided singling out Johnson for blame. Kennedy spoke of the tradition of dissent, citing Abraham Lincoln's opposition to the Mexican War, and commented on the historical role of the Senate in debating war and peace. Although he still opposed a unilateral American withdrawal from Vietnam, conceding it would be "a repudiation of commitments undertaken and confirmed by three administrations," he nonetheless challenged the administration to live up to its oft-stated desire for a peaceful resolution.

Kennedy called for a "middle way" between unilateral withdrawal and military victory. "Whatever the exact status of the National Liberation Front—puppet or partly independent," he said:

> any negotiated settlement must accept the fact that there are discontented elements in South Viet Nam, Communist and non-Communist, who desire to change the existing political and economic system of the country. There are three things you can do with such groups: kill or repress them, turn the country over to them, or admit them to a share of power and responsibility. The first two are now possible only through force of arms.

The only alternative, in Kennedy's view, was to give the NLF "a share of power and responsibility," which was "at the heart of the hope for a negotiated settlement." *"It may mean a compromise government fully acceptable to neither side,"* he added, but "we must be willing to face the uncertainties of election, and the possibility of an eventual vote on reunification." [emphasis in original]

Kennedy was oblivious to the possibility that his remarks would touch off a public confrontation with senior administration officials. That morning he was probably thinking more about joining his wife, Ethel, for a ski weekend in Stowe, Vermont, than about the stir his comments might cause in Washington. The next day "RFK Wants Viet Reds In Coalition" read some headlines, and the *Chicago Tribune* ran the story under the simple headline: "Ho Chi Kennedy." Coming on the heels of the "blood for the Viet Cong" controversy and his defense of the rights of draft resisters, this latest blast had a chilling effect.

After hearing about Kennedy's remarks, Vice President Hubert Humphrey told reporters: "I do not believe we should write a prescription for Viet Nam which includes a dose of arsenic." Kennedy's call to include the NLF in a political settlement, he said, would be "like having a fox in the chicken coop" or "an arsonist in the fire department." Humphrey called the NLF a "stooge" of Hanoi. Kennedy's words reverberated all the way to Southeast Asia. South Vietnam's new prime minister, Air Vice Marshal Nguyen Cao Ky, was furious: "The so-called National Liberation Front does not liberate anybody," he snapped to reporters in Saigon. "They killed 11,000 of our troops last year and 22,000 of the innocent people in the countryside. They murdered them. They are 1,000 percent Communist and they are illegal, so let's not talk about the National Liberation Front anymore."

In an attempt to defend himself, Kennedy cut short his ski vacation to appear on *Face the Nation*. "I think that statements that are made that we will never deal with assassins and we will never deal with murderers," he said, referring to some of Humphrey's comments, "make it difficult for them [the Vietcong] to believe that they are being asked to the negotiating table other than to surrender." For the next three days, Kennedy's stand on the NLF was the center of surprisingly intense media coverage. The next day Kennedy appeared on NBC's *Today Show* to further clarify his position. Despite trying to cool the dispute, he remained firm in his conviction that "the dissident elements" in South Vietnam "must be brought into any peace talks." The United States' "political objectives should be absolutely clear," he insisted. "If we want to destroy the Viet Cong we should be prepared for a long and bloody fight which eventually may bring in China."

As the week wore on, Kennedy backed off from his original statement and contended he was closer to the administration's view than the press had understood. Kennedy's "clarifications" satisfied neither his peace movement allies nor his pro-war critics and resulted in a political embarrassment. Feeling burned, he learned that he would have to be far more cautious when offering his advice on the Vietnam War.

Cold War liberals of the 89th and 90th Congresses, including Kennedy, had to couch their criticisms of the war in positive terms. Coming down too hard on Johnson for his foreign policy could impede the historic progress he was making in the domestic field, which included sweeping legislation affecting civil rights, health care (Medicare and Medicaid), education, and antipoverty programs. Further, President Johnson appeared to have a prescription for success in Vietnam. He weighed his military options carefully and displayed restraint. In 1965 and early 1966, it seemed that Johnson might achieve his stated goal: propping up a pro-U.S. government in Saigon. Although Kennedy had predicted privately in the summer of 1965 that the war could become a liability for Johnson, possibly blocking his domestic agenda, the President remained a popular figure.

7

Senator Kennedy, the Cautious Critic

The Canadian government had named the highest unclimbed peak in North America after President John F. Kennedy, and when the National Geographic Society suggested that the surviving Kennedy brothers scale it, Robert Kennedy felt compelled to meet the challenge. He enjoyed sailing, riding rapids, swimming in the ocean, and skiing, so it was not surprising that he agreed to become the first person to conquer 14,000-foot Mount Kennedy. (Edward Kennedy was still recuperating from back injuries from his June 1964 plane crash, but he probably would have passed on it anyway.) Kennedy enlisted Jim Whittaker, the first American to climb Mount Everest, to be his guide, which sparked a lasting friendship between the two adventurers. Over the course of the next 18 months, Kennedy's political battles with President Johnson over the Vietnam War would seem at times even more arduous than conquering a mountain, but he continued to learn about the world and his place in it with several important trips abroad.

The only regimen Kennedy followed to prepare for the mountain climb was to run up and down the stairs at Hickory Hill. Whittaker wondered if he was up to the task. But in March 1965, when they left the base camp at 8,700 feet for the final ascent, roped together at the waist, Whittaker was impressed with Kennedy's pace and determination. After two days of nearly vertical climbing, the veteran mountaineer guided Kennedy to a spot about 50 yards below the summit and let him traverse the rest of the way alone. Kennedy reached the mountaintop and kneeled down; he crossed himself and planted into the snow two flags: an American flag and one with the Kennedy family crest. He also carefully buried a handful of PT 109 tie clips and a copy of President Kennedy's inaugural address. Later, when Kennedy returned home, he confided to friends: "I'm glad that I did it, and I'm glad that it's over." The press widely reported the expedition, which enhanced Kennedy's image as a man of daring and action, and before the end of the year, he made another well-publicized trip, this time to Latin America.

In November 1965, Kennedy traveled to several nations on the continent to the south. In Chile, after being warned that leftist students were going to shout him down if he spoke at a university in Concepción, Kennedy showed up anyway. An unruly crowd of mostly Communist youths hurled garbage and eggs at him, and one student even spat in his face when Kennedy reached out to shake his hand. Still Kennedy earned the respect of many Chilean students that day for being willing to listen to their views. Also in Chile, he arrived unannounced early in the morning at a copper mine where miners were paid less than $1.25 a day. Kennedy ignored the manager, who begged him not to go, and then "jumped, headfirst, into a mining car going into the darkest depths of the mine." When he reemerged, Kennedy proclaimed: "If I worked in these mines I'd be a Communist too." Kennedy's thinking was evolving about the social forces at work that produced insurgent movements in Latin America, and he was developing a new empathy with those who suffered under unjust conditions.

In Lima, Peru, he told a student audience: "The responsibility of our times is nothing less than a revolution. . . . We can affect its character; we cannot alter its inevitability." He began expressing sentiments similar to those of President Kennedy, who said: "Those who make nonviolent revolution impossible, make violent revolution inevitable." He even said he admired the idealism of the continent's most notorious revolutionary: Che Guevara. He tried to reach out to young people wherever he went. On November 20, he celebrated his 40th birthday in Brazil, and two days later he honored the anniversary of his brother's assassination by leaping out of vehicles in the poor neighborhoods of Sao Paulo, yelling to the crowds: "Every child an education! Every family adequate housing! Every man a job!" Kennedy had come a long way from his days as an anti-Castro zealot. He was beginning to see the world less as an epic struggle between East and West and more as a complex and nuanced set of human relationships. He was becoming more familiar with the social injustices that ordinary people faced around the world, and his views on the subject continued to evolve as they had for millions of other Americans in the 1960s.

When Kennedy returned to Washington, he outlined his ideas for U.S.–Latin American relations. In a lengthy, two-part statement presented on the Senate floor, he urged support for those working for democracy and reform in the hemisphere: "The responsibility of our time is nothing less than to lead a revolution, a revolution which will be peaceful if we are wise enough, whether we will it or not." Kennedy now argued that without comprehensive reform, or worse still, if the United States played its historical role of using its power to prop up oligarchies and military juntas, "the ignored and dispossessed, the insulted and injured" will turn to Communism as "the only way out of their misery." He called for doubling the amount of U.S. aid: "an equivalent for all Latin America of the cost of approximately four weeks of the struggle in Vietnam." Kennedy's views had shifted considerably from the time of Operation Mongoose, and his trip to Latin America was an eye-opening experience. As the 1960s progressed, the élan of the period, defined by the outpouring of citizen activism against injustice, began to profoundly affect him.

During his first 18 months in the Senate, Kennedy avoided clashes with the Johnson administration over Vietnam. Instead, he concentrated on domestic issues. He believed Johnson's "Great Society" programs had paid too little attention to job creation. Johnson had signed more legislation protecting the rights of workers and consumers and enlarging the fields of health care and education for more Americans than any other President since Franklin Roosevelt. Kennedy supported the goals of the Great Society, but he criticized Johnson's antipoverty agenda for spending money without requiring contributions from local businesses and the wealthy. He remained committed to New Deal liberalism, but he saw some social programs as being wasteful, unsustainable, and likely to breed dependency. He had faith in government action to alleviate poverty, but he remained skeptical of large bureaucracies doling out relief. The riots in black urban centers of the preceding two summers influenced Kennedy's views on poverty and how combustible the atmosphere had become. It would be a grave mistake, he argued, "to limit our efforts to the support of the war in Vietnam" and "postpone action on our pressing domestic needs." Diverting America's attention away from its long-festering social inequality, Kennedy believed, "would be to invite the very internal conflagration of which we have been warned—to invite a society so irretrievably split that no war will be worth fighting, and no war will be possible to fight."

The free market system had clearly failed impoverished communities because there was little financial incentive for it to do otherwise, and Kennedy set out to change that. He wanted to utilize the federal tax code to encourage the private sector to invest in economically depressed areas. His views on alleviating poverty blended government activism with an emphasis on self-reliance. Kennedy asked a simple question: What will these programs look like in 20 years? Without creating jobs, in his view their failure was almost assured.

In early 1966, Kennedy entered the national antipoverty debate in a big way by launching a Special Impact Program for the Bedford-Stuyvesant section of Brooklyn. He often walked the streets of "Bed-Sty," an impoverished neighborhood that was home to over 400,000 residents, 84 percent African American and 16 percent Puerto Rican. He was appalled by the unemployment, vacant lots, and empty storefronts. He envisioned a long-term project that would revitalize the city by luring jobs to the area and allowing members of the community to participate at every level. He hoped it would become a model for other self-sustaining efforts to rebuild blighted urban centers.

"No government program now operating," Kennedy said, "gives any substantial promise of meeting the unemployment crisis." He cited government statistics indicating that in many cities almost 75 percent of young African Americans were unemployed. In 1965, only 3 percent of the 950,000 jobs created for youth had gone to blacks. Referring to Johnson's Great Society, Kennedy said: "There is not a problem for which money is not being spent. There is not a problem or a program on which dozens or hundreds or thousands of bureaucrats are not earnestly at work. But does this represent a solution to our problems? Manifestly it does not."

Kennedy wrested from Congress start-up money for the Bed-Sty project and enlisted the help of businesses as well as state and municipal governments. He brought together Democrats and Republicans, including Mayor John Lindsay of New York City and the senior senator from New York, Jacob Javits. He also recruited former Treasury Secretary Douglas Dillon (after whom Kennedy would name one of his children) and IBM chairman Thomas Watson, who was one of Kennedy's few noteworthy allies in the business world.

To implement the program, Kennedy created two complementary organizations: the Bedford-Stuyvesant Renewal and Rehabilitation

Corporation, which was controlled by the community, and the Development and Services Corporation, which included private investors from outside the community. "We are all in this together," he said, unveiling the project at an event with Mayor Lindsay and Senator Javits by his side. "Today on this platform and in this room, there are Democrats and Republicans, white and black, businessmen and government officials, rich and poor, and people from every part of this varied community. This is a unique effort—the only one of its kind and scope in the country. . . . We are going to try, as few have tried before not just to have programs like others have, but to create new kinds of systems for education and health and employment and housing. We here are going to see, in fact, whether the city and its people, with the cooperation of government and private business and foundations, can meet the challenge of urban life in the last third of the twentieth century."

It was an ambitious task with many setbacks, but within the next few years, Bedford-Stuyvesant experienced renewed development. A community center and 300 new homes were built, and IBM delivered on its promise to create several hundred new jobs in the community. Poverty was far from eradicated in Bed-Sty, but the people in the community participated in making it a better place to live. The project served as a model for partnerships in other poverty zones. *Newsweek* magazine dubbed it "the most sweeping and comprehensive rehabilitation effort ever brought to bear on a single American community." The venture in Bed-Sty was consistent with Kennedy's views of work and relief: "We cannot afford to continue, year after year, the increases in welfare costs which result when a substantial segment of the population becomes permanently unemployable," he said. "We cannot afford the loss of the tax revenue we would receive if these people were jobholders. Our slums are too expensive. We cannot afford them."

While he launched his new project in Brooklyn, Kennedy also worked with the Subcommittee on Migrant Labor, which led to a lasting bond with César Chávez and the union he co-founded, the United Farm Workers (UFW). In March 1966, Kennedy traveled to Delano, California, to hold hearings on the violent struggles between California's powerful agribusiness interests and the largely Mexican immigrants who harvested the fruits and vegetables destined for America's dinner tables. Chávez was a tireless labor organizer and a Latino cultural leader who had mobilized about 13,000 of the most oppressed workers in the country. The minimum wage laws did not apply to them, and they worked long hours with short-handled hoes, living in shacks near pesticide-laden fields. The local landowners claimed Chávez and the union were all "Communists." They hired private security guards to disrupt the UFW's organizing activities, beat up workers, and create a climate of intimidation. At the time of Kennedy's visit, the union was in the middle of a bitter strike and grape boycott against California's politically powerful growers. Chávez and his union sought elementary rights that other American workers had taken for granted since the 1930s, such as the right to form an independent union and to collectively bargain.

Kennedy presided over a raucous hearing during which he heard testimony from dozens of farm workers who spoke of brutal treatment by the landlords, vigilantes, and law enforcement. When a local police chief testified that sheriffs routinely arrested picketers to prevent the possibility of a riot, Kennedy grew livid: "This is the most interesting concept. How can you go arrest somebody if they haven't violated the law?" he asked. "I suggest that during the luncheon period that the sheriff and the district attorney read the Constitution of the United States." When Kennedy returned to the Senate, he called for extending all of the federal labor protections to migrant laborers, and he became the UFW's staunchest ally inside the government. He was growing more aware of the social injustices that confronted working people both at home and abroad.

Another eye-opening trip for Kennedy came in June 1966, when he traveled to South Africa, a nation that was then a white supremacist "apartheid" state. Over 22 million South African blacks languished in densely populated "bantustans," which resembled Indian reservations. About 5 million whites (and some people of "mixed race") controlled the economy, the government, and the best lands. Apartheid, the legal system that separated blacks from whites, was codified in 1948 but was, in fact, a product of decades of colonialism. There were stark similarities between apartheid and the Jim Crow system in the American South. The apartheid regime had outlawed the major black political organization, the African National Congress (ANC), and had arrested or "banned" with house arrest many of its leaders, including Nelson Mandela and Nobel Peace Prize recipient Chief Albert Luthuli.

Kennedy visited South Africa at a pivotal moment in that nation's history. The years of civil rights victories in the American South had given renewed determination to those who challenged apartheid. The National Union of South African Students (NUSAS), which was trying to break down the racial barriers, had invited Kennedy. The South African government denied travel visas to 40 members of the press who planned to accompany Robert and Ethel Kennedy, and government officials refused to meet with him. Five days before Kennedy arrived, the South African government "banned" the president of NUSAS, Ian Robertson. When he arrived, Kennedy defied the government and met privately with Chief Luthuli and with Robertson at his home to offer his encouragement. He showed Robertson how to dislodge listening devices by jumping up and down on the wooden floor, a trick Kennedy had learned while he was attorney general.

On June 6, 1966, on a cold South African winter day, Kennedy gave the keynote address for the "Day of Affirmation," speaking to an audience of 15,000 at the University of Cape Town. The auditorium was filled to capacity, and students set up loud speakers outside the building so the thousands of people who gathered could listen. When Kennedy started speaking, government security agents snipped the speaker wires. He opened his remarks by telling the crowd that the Union of South African and the United States of America had similar histories; both nations had populations that settled a new land and created prosperous economies, but they also had displaced the indigenous people and suffered from racism and inequality. "Few will have the greatness to bend history itself," he told the racially integrated audience, "but each of us can work to change a small portion of events, and in the total of all those acts will be written the history of this generation."

> It is from numberless diverse acts of courage and belief that human history is shaped. Each time a man stands up for an ideal, or acts to improve the lot of others, or strikes out against injustice, he sends forth a tiny ripple of hope, and crossing each other from a million different centers of energy and daring those ripples build a current which can sweep down the mightiest walls of oppression and resistance. . . . And everyone here will ultimately be judged—will ultimately judge himself—on the effort he has contributed to building a new world society and the extent to which his ideals and goals have shaped that effort.

Kennedy toured South African townships in open cars, shaking the outstretched hands of children, men, and women. "I wish we had two more days in South Africa," he wrote a friend. "By the last day I was speaking on street corners on the back of a car—and people believed." While he was visiting the impoverished black township of Soweto, James Meredith was shot and wounded in Mississippi after he embarked on his solo March Against Fear. In a speech before a crowd of 7,000 at the University of Witwatersrand, Kennedy drew powerful comparisons between the racism Meredith faced in the American South and that of South Africa. When he returned, he visited Meredith in the hospital. Kennedy's speeches during his visit to South Africa profoundly resonated with a new generation of antiapartheid activists. He returned home with a better understanding of racism and resistance.

That fall Kennedy traversed the United States speaking at fundraisers for Democratic candidates who were running in the midterm elections. Virtually all of the mainstream politicians supported President Johnson and the war in Vietnam. During the 1966 campaign season, a small group calling itself "Citizens for Kennedy" emerged. Headed by Martin Shepard, a 32-year-old Manhattan psychiatrist, the organization sent out mailers to Democrats, purchased anti-war advertisements in newspapers, and prodded Kennedy to take a tougher stand against the war. It claimed to have 7,500 members.

When he appeared in public, Kennedy often found himself surrounded by peace activists and people urging him to run for President. It was not uncommon for crowds to greet him with signs reading: "BOBBY IN '68; BOBBY IN '72; BOBBY ANYTIME!" A typical headline read: "Crowds Applaud LBJ, Squeal at Kennedy." In October 1966, Kennedy predicted in a letter to his eldest son, Joseph, that the Democrats would "do reasonably well perhaps losing about 30 seats in the House of Representatives which is not too bad in an off year." His solicitous correspondence with his 13-year-old son, who was then at Milton Academy, probably arose from Kennedy's own childhood experience of always trying to elicit his father's notice. "The party in power always loses some," he explained, "and with the majorities that the Democrats have in Congress you could expect to lose at least 30 seats." (The Democrats lost 47 seats in the House that year but held onto their majority.)

By the end of 1966, Kennedy felt boxed in by the war issue. The growing peace movement demanded that he take bolder action, while the pro-war Democratic leadership urged him to stay quiet lest he divide the party. "If I become convinced that by making another speech that I could do some good, I would make it tomorrow,"

Kennedy told a friend. "But the last time I spoke I didn't have any influence on policy, and I was hurt politically. I'm afraid that by speaking out I just make Lyndon do the opposite, out of spite. He hates me so much that if I asked for snow, he would make rain, just because it was me." At about that same time, Kennedy met with wounded servicemen who had returned from Vietnam at a Queens naval hospital. Allard Lowenstein, the New York peace activist who accompanied him, recalled that "it was very clear how deeply the war bothered him even before he made many public statements about it." But Kennedy's caution on the war drew bitter criticism from some people who were active in the peace movement.

In early February 1967, Kennedy made a quick trip to Europe, mainly to assess the negative effects the Vietnam War was having in the centers of power in England, Germany, Italy, and France. He met with British Prime Minister Harold Wilson, German Chancellor Kurt Kiesinger, and Italian Premier Aldo Moro. In Paris, he conferred with French Foreign Ministry officials who were knowledgeable about Vietnam. President Charles DeGaulle talked about the political corruption in Saigon and expressed his contempt for South Vietnam's rulers. In one meeting, the director of Asian affairs for the French Foreign Ministry, Etienne Manach, informed Kennedy that Hanoi had changed its negotiating position. North Vietnam wanted Kennedy to know that Ho Chi Minh was willing to enter into direct talks with the United States while the status of the NLF was temporarily shelved. At first, Kennedy was unaware that he had received information on a major new breakthrough.

The press caught wind of the episode, and it was quickly disseminated that Kennedy had received a "peace feeler" while he was in Europe, an overture from Hanoi that had eluded the Johnson administration. When he came home and reporters asked him about the "peace feeler," Kennedy was baffled: "I return from Europe hopeful about peace but without any 'feelers,'" he said. Seeking to clarify the matter, he requested a meeting with President Johnson. On February 6, 1967, Kennedy and Johnson met in the White House. Accounts of the meeting vary in the biographical works on Kennedy. His legislative assistant, Peter Edelman, said that Kennedy appeared "shaken" after the encounter; he heard that Johnson had been "very, very crude and angry and swore at Kennedy." Kennedy's press secretary, Frank Mankiewicz, said that, when Kennedy called for Johnson to expand the role of the International Control Commission to monitor a cease-fire in South Vietnam, the President cut him off in midsentence, saying: "Well, I want you to know that I'm not going to adopt any single one of those suggestions because we're going to win the war, and you doves will all be dead in six months."

As with the controversy a year earlier, when he first called for reevaluation of the role of the NLF, Kennedy once again found himself burned politically and on the defensive. This time, however, he decided to respond with his first major address on the war in over a year. On March 2, 1967, Kennedy walked into the Senate chamber and delivered a lengthy, carefully worded speech on finding a way out of Vietnam. At the time of his presentation, the United States had already committed 400,000 combat troops, and there had been over 5,500 Americans killed. Present were Senator J. William Fulbright, the chair of the Foreign Relations Committee, and 19 other senators.

Kennedy stopped short of calling for a unilateral withdrawal of U.S. forces, which had been the peace movement's position. He offered a mea culpa for his own role in escalating the conflict during his brother's presidency: "I can testify that if fault is to be found or responsibility assessed, there is enough to go round for all—including myself." Although he acknowledged "nearly all Americans share with us the determination and intention to remain in Vietnam until we have fulfilled our commitments," he criticized the war for "diverting resources which might have been used to help eliminate American poverty, improve the education of our children and enhance the quality of our national life." The operative paragraph, which Mankiewicz distributed as a press release, stated: "I propose that we test the sincerity of the statements by [Soviet] Premier [Aleksei] Kosygin and others asserting that if the bombardment of the North is halted, negotiations would begin—by halting the bombardment and saying we are ready to negotiate within the week; making it clear that discussions cannot continue for a prolonged period without an agreement that neither side will substantially increase the size of the war in South Vietnam by infiltration or reinforcement."

Kennedy also called for an expanded role for the United Nations with the aim of removing the United States as a unilateral military force in Vietnam. He again suggested that the NLF be included in the politics of South Vietnam, which he saw as the only realistic alternative, given the organization's mass base. "All the people of South Vietnam," he said, "communist and non-communist, Buddhist and Christian, should be able to choose their leaders, and seek office through peaceful political processes, free from external coercion and internal violence." Finally, he called for the United States to unconditionally cease the bombing, which is why it became known as Kennedy's "Stop the Bombing" speech.

When Johnson heard about the speech, he brandished to aides a fistful of newspaper clippings that documented Kennedy's inconsistent statements on the war. Polls showed that 67 percent of the American people still favored bombing North Vietnam and that Kennedy's remarks had a negligible effect. The nation had not yet reached the level of opposition to the war that would become evident a year later. Peace activists welcomed Kennedy's "Stop the Bombing" address, but critics faulted him for not calling for a unilateral withdrawal of U.S. troops and for remaining open to future military action if the negotiations were derailed. Still Kennedy nudged the mainstream debate closer to the dove position, and his views were consistent with those of America's European allies.

On March 7, 1967, Kennedy found himself in the public hot seat once again when he appeared on NBC's *Today Show*. Two of the nation's most well known political commentators, Sander Vanocur and Hugh Downs, grilled him about his rivalry with Johnson. It was entertaining television to frame the Vietnam policy differences between the President and the late President's brother as a duel between two strong-willed individuals. The interviewers focused on whether the speech helped or hindered Kennedy's pursuit of the presidency in 1972. "I don't think really the questions of personalities should enter into this matter," Kennedy said, trying to deflect them. "I think [the war is] of far greater importance. I know that President Johnson is a man of peace. I know that he wants to find an end to this struggle in Vietnam. I have perhaps some different ideas as to what should be done." In the televised interview, Kennedy tried to direct the discussion back to his ideas about ending the war. He came off as being sincere, though somewhat inarticulate. He sometimes stuttered and punctuated his remarks with awkward pauses; he possessed none of the polish and ease with the medium for which his brother was famous. But RFK possessed a raw authenticity that television amplified.

The interviewers asked Kennedy if his criticism of the war would hurt the Democrats. He responded by saying that he believed Vietnam was "far more important and transcends any loyalty to one's own political party." They asked him why he had chosen this moment to make the speech. "I thought we were at a critical time," he answered. "And before we take the final plunge to even greater escalation, I think that we should try negotiation. If we can't find the answer to it, we can always go back to the war." When they fired off the utterly presumptuous question about whether he planned to try to strip Johnson of the nomination in 1968, Kennedy, clearly flummoxed, replied: "No, I mean, I'm going to support President Johnson, and I'm going to support Vice President Humphrey, and I would expect that the rest of the Democratic Party would do likewise. And I would be glad, if they feel it would help, I'll be glad to campaign."

Kennedy's "Stop the Bombing" speech was probably the strongest he could make without fueling the growing divisions inside the party and jeopardizing his long-term political ambitions. However, these calculations did not completely paralyze him; he continued to call for nonmilitary solutions to the conflict. "I think our own country's split," he said, "and I think there's also been a decline of our own leadership around the world because of the war in Vietnam. I found it in South America. I found it in Africa, and I found it just recently and most dramatically in Europe." Although Kennedy failed to score political points, his criticism gave legitimacy to the war's opponents, and he extended the parameters of acceptable dissent. At the very least, his latest critique helped create a new environment where other public figures had greater freedom to raise their voices against the war.

8

Coming Out Against the Vietnam War

A month after Kennedy's "Stop the Bombing" speech, Martin Luther King, Jr., defied warnings from moderate civil rights leaders and broke with President Johnson over the war in Vietnam. On April 4, 1967, at the Riverside Church in New York City, King denounced the war at an event sponsored by Clergy and Laity Concerned About Vietnam (CALCAV). For years, peace activists urged the 1964 Nobel Peace Prize laureate to join them, but King refrained from doing so because he feared it would alienate Johnson, who had been his ally in passing landmark civil rights legislation. By the spring of 1967, however, King concluded he could not fight for social justice at home while the United States fought an unjust war abroad. "I speak as a citizen of the world," he said, "for the world stands aghast at the path we have taken. I speak as an American to the leaders of my own nation. The great initiative in this war is ours. The initiative to stop must be ours." Throughout 1967, Kennedy found himself on the same trajectory as King in voicing ever-stronger opposition to the Vietnam War.

King's proposals for peace mirrored Kennedy's, but his role as a spiritual leader and his oratorical skills enabled him to draw the lines with greater eloquence and moral clarity. In 1967, King's role in American politics was unique. He had become world famous for leading the nonviolent African-American struggle in the South, and he had built a network of alliances with the major religious denominations. The organization he founded, the Southern Christian Leadership Conference (SCLC), had become a lightning rod for social activism. At the age of 38, King had already carved out his place among the pantheon of America's greatest leaders.

Some of King's civil rights allies opposed his linking their cause with the waste of lives and money in Vietnam. They feared it would poison their relationship with the President and the Congress. Johnson had signed two of the most sweeping laws affecting African Americans since Reconstruction: the Civil Rights Act of 1964 and the Voting Rights Act of 1965. The Voting Rights Act was the crowning achievement of the civil rights movement, and it had been passed after a bitter struggle in Selma, Alabama.

On March 7, 1965, "Bloody Sunday," Alabama troopers attacked voting rights protesters on the Edmund Pettus Bridge as they began a nonviolent march from Selma to Montgomery. Two other marches followed, with participants protected by federal troops. Johnson signed the Voting Rights Act five months later. It provided vital federal protections that enabled blacks in the South to register to vote and to participate in fair elections.

Challenging Johnson on the war could hinder the historic progress that African Americans were making. King understood his colleagues' concerns; "others can do what they want to do," he said. But his conscience compelled him to denounce the bloodshed. He was particularly critical of the $20 billion earmarked for the war in 1967, which dwarfed the money spent on domestic antipoverty programs. King pointed out that the United States spent over $100,000 for each enemy killed in Vietnam, while it spent about $50 on each American in poverty. He also denounced, as did Kennedy, the disproportionate number of black soldiers who were fighting and dying in Southeast Asia.

The president of the National Association for the Advancement of Colored People (NAACP), Roy Wilkins, and the head of the Urban League, Whitney Young, distanced their organizations from King after his Vietnam speech. Retired baseball legend Jackie Robinson, the first black player in the Major League, and African-American Senator Edward Brooke of Massachusetts criticized King's stand. Editorialists in *The New York Times*, *Life* magazine, and other influential journals called King's break with Johnson a "mistake." *Time* magazine called the speech "demagogic slander that sounded like a script for Radio Hanoi." *The Washington Post* concluded: "King has diminished his usefulness to his cause, his country, his people." King instantly became the most important leader of the peace movement.

The same month King broke with Johnson, Kennedy traveled to rural Mississippi with an entourage of African-American activists who had close ties to King and the SCLC. After hearing testimony to a Senate Committee about the crushing poverty in Mississippi from Marian Wright, a 27-year-old Yale Law School graduate who worked for the NAACP's Legal Defense and Educational Fund, Kennedy wanted to see for himself. He toured the Mississippi Delta with civil rights veterans, including Fannie Lou Hamer, the founder of the Mississippi Freedom Democratic Party, which had unsuccessfully challenged the all-white Mississippi delegation at the 1964 Democratic National Convention, and Charles Evers, the brother of slain NAACP official Medgar Evers. Kennedy was stunned to see malnutrition and poverty on par with South Africa and Latin America in the United States.

Marian Wright described the scene at one Mississippi hamlet they visited: "Without cameras we went inside a very dark and dank shack. It was filthy and very poor. There was a child sitting on a dirt floor, filthy." Kennedy "got down on his knees and he tried to talk to the child and get a response," she said. He sat on the floor, holding the little girl, who was clearly undernourished, rocking her back and forth. The listless child gave Kennedy no reaction, and he was visibly shaken by the encounter. Writes biographer Evan Thomas, Kennedy was "highly agitated when he returned to Washington that night." His eldest daughter, Kathleen, recalled that her father was "ashen faced." He told his nine children, ages 2 to 15, who were eating dinner: "In Mississippi a whole family lives in a shack the size of this room. Do you know how lucky you are?" When he resumed his work in the Senate, Kennedy demanded from the Department of Agriculture emergency food assistance for those areas of the South most in need. He also sought appropriations from Congress for sustained federal aid.

Meantime Allard Lowenstein recruited Martin Luther King, Jr., to help lead the Spring Mobilization Against the War. The peace movement had coalesced under an umbrella organization called the Mobilization Committee to End the Vietnam War (known as "the Mobe"). The group brought together opponents of the war from diverse backgrounds and ideologies and organized the first large-scale demonstrations in New York City and San Francisco. Lowenstein used the momentum of the Spring Mobilization to launch Vietnam Summer, which sent out a small army of student peace activists to knock on doors in dozens of cities. Vietnam Summer was modeled after the 1964 Freedom Summer project, when nearly four hundred volunteers walked precincts throughout Mississippi to register black voters. The movement to end the Vietnam War was finally becoming a force in national politics.

Lowenstein and other activists enlisted as many prominent voices against the war as they could, and they constantly pushed Kennedy to join them and take a bolder stand. But on June 3, 1967, in New York City, Kennedy disheartened the peace movement when he introduced President Johnson at a Democratic fund-raiser. At the Americana Hotel, Kennedy gave Johnson what *The New York Times* described as "perhaps the warmest endorsement the Senator has ever offered." Outside the hotel, over 1,400 people protested, including one couple who held placards depicting LBJ in a Nazi uniform with the words "Wanted for Murder." There was also a contingent from the Peace Corps with signs reading "Stop Bombing the Schools We Helped Build."

Inside the plush banquet room, Kennedy was sandwiched between Johnson and Vice President Hubert Humphrey. He began his remarks by citing the dictionary definition of the word "greatness" and attributed it to Johnson. "The height of his aim, the breadth of his achievement, the record of his past, and the promises of his future," Kennedy gushed. Johnson had led "this nation at a time of uncertainty and danger, pouring out his own strength to renew the strength and the purpose of all the people of this nation." He went on to lavish a string of accolades on the President, and the 1,600 New York City Democrats who had paid $100 each to attend the dinner gave him a friendly ovation.

But when the media disseminated Kennedy's remarks, the episode marked a low point of his relationship with the peace movement. New York journalist Jimmy Breslin wrote that during the Spring Mobilization 250,000 people had marched in the city and "Lyndon Johnson was a name marchers used only to frighten children." Now Kennedy showered him with praise. Anti-war activists were dumbfounded that Kennedy would close ranks with the President, and his words resurrected the old charge of "opportunism." Arthur Schlesinger, Jr., who was becoming more critical of the war, attributed Kennedy's over-the-top tribute to a single "hyperbolic paragraph" that Theodore Sorensen had inserted into his speech. Two weeks later Schlesinger wrote Kennedy: "I think you have made only one mistake and that is your remarks at the dinner in New York about LBJ. They seemed out of character, and that is one thing you must never do."

Despite his stand on the war and his animosity toward Johnson, Kennedy believed that political necessity dictated that he remain loyal to the President. But his cozying up to the party leadership did not stop Citizens for Kennedy from sending out recruiting letters calling for him to run in 1968. "With Johnson we lose," one letter stated. "We voted against Goldwater, but we find ourselves saddled with his foreign policy anyway. Johnson means defeat for the Democrats in '68. But with Robert F. Kennedy, we have a candidate who can win." Kennedy sent out mailers disavowing Citizens for Kennedy.

In July 1967, while Kennedy tried to prevent his feelings about the war from interfering with his long-term political goals, the African-American section of Detroit exploded in a week of rioting that left 43 dead and over 1,000 injured. There were 7,000 people held in makeshift detention centers and $50 million in destroyed property. The situation was so out of control that not even the Michigan National Guard could quell the violence. Republican Governor George Romney had to ask President Johnson to deploy federal troops, and Johnson sent in the 82nd Airborne.

The Detroit riot, like the violence in South Central Los Angeles two years earlier, rekindled the debate between those who called for restoring "law and order" and those who wished to address the underlying social causes of the riots. The commissions formed to study the violence pointed to black unemployment, endemic poverty, "urban renewal" projects that devastated black neighborhoods, the "redlining" of blacks into specific zones, and brutality from white police departments as setting the stage for the unrest. The urban violence, which engulfed not only Los Angeles and Detroit but also dozens of other cities, revealed that, despite African-American gains and Johnson's antipoverty programs, America's cities remained hotbeds of racial tension.

The destruction in the cities shifted the spotlight of the civil rights movement away from racial integration in the South to the uncharted territory of black economic empowerment in the cities of the North and West. Martin Luther King, Jr., sought to channel what he called the "misguided" energy of the riots into nonviolent action that could move the country away from racial polarization. He mobilized his supporters to attack the complex problems of urban poverty and racism with nonviolent direct action.

In November 1967, King launched the Poor People's Campaign, which he hoped would organize thousands of the nation's destitute people of all races to march to Washington, D.C. King's Poor People's Campaign envisioned a class-based, nonviolent movement that would demand a "domestic Marshall Plan" of $30 billion to fight poverty. "As we work to get rid of the economic strangulation that we face as a result of poverty," King wrote, "we must not overlook the fact that millions of Puerto Ricans, Mexican Americans, Indians, and Appalachian whites are also poverty stricken. Any serious war against poverty must of necessity include them." King envisioned the culminating event of the campaign to be larger than the 1963 March on Washington.

Kennedy welcomed the Poor People's Campaign and embraced its goals as a nonviolent alternative to the growing unrest in the cities. Marian Wright, who had brought Kennedy to Mississippi (and later married Kennedy aide Peter Edelman), said that Kennedy's critique of poverty in America had played a role in King's decision to organize the new march on Washington. King was going to marshal the poor to be a voice in the electoral politics of 1968.

In November 1967, Kennedy published *To Seek a Newer World*, which drew its title from a line in a Tennyson poem: "Come, my friends. T'is not too late to seek a newer world." The book was a compilation of Kennedy's speeches on the Vietnam War, race relations, and foreign policy. It was the type of book a person who was thinking about running for President would write. In *To Seek a Newer World*, Kennedy again called for ending the bombing of North Vietnam and for incorporating the NLF into the political life of South Vietnam. Two anti-war groups, the Committee for a Sane Nuclear Policy (SANE) and CALCAV, which had sponsored King's Riverside Church address, distributed excerpts of *To Seek a Newer World* as anti-war pamphlets. *Look* magazine also published Kennedy's essay on Vietnam.

In *To Seek a Newer World*, Kennedy once again acknowledged his personal role in contributing to the Vietnam catastrophe: "I am willing to bear my share of the responsibility before history and before my fellow citizens" because "past error is no excuse for its own perpetuation." He quoted from Sophocles' *Antigone*: "All men make mistakes, but a good man yields when he knows his course is wrong, and repairs the evil." Kennedy's repeated mea culpas for his role in widening the war during his brother's administration seem to reflect a need to assuage his personal guilt.

When his book came out, Kennedy also escalated his anti-war rhetoric, saying on one Sunday talk show: "We're killing South Vietnamese, we're killing children, we're killing women, we're killing innocent people because we don't want to have the war fought on American soil, or because they're 12,000 miles away and they might get to be 11,000 miles away." He said there were "35,000 people without limbs in South Vietnam" and "150,000 civilian casualties every year." "When we use napalm," he continued, "when a village is destroyed and civilians are killed, this is a moral obligation and a moral responsibility for us here in the United States." Kennedy's pointed criticism raised expectations among those who hoped he would challenge Johnson as a peace candidate in 1968. Citizens for Kennedy again took out full-page ads in newspapers demanding that he run.

The Democratic Party was becoming bitterly divided on the Vietnam War. James Farley, a former chairman of the party's national committee and a Johnson ally, blasted Kennedy at a regional conference in Salt Lake City. Speaking for the leadership, Farley told an audience of Democratic officials that he felt "pity for the junior Senator from New York." He said that Kennedy suffered from "political vertigo because his party and his president elevated him too fast" and that he was "urging a Bay of Pigs run-out on a world scale." Farley said that Kennedy violated a "solemn promise" that Truman, Eisenhower, and JFK had made that "the people of Vietnam would not be deserted." While Farley spoke, Kennedy's supporters who were present hung their heads like children being scolded.

In late 1967, Allard Lowenstein, who had put together the Spring Mobilization and Vietnam Summer, began organizing a Dump Johnson movement for the 1968 presidential primaries. Kennedy was the first person he asked to lead the effort. Lowenstein and Citizens for Kennedy wanted to strip the New York senator of the luxury of remaining outside the fray. "Either Lyndon Johnson must abandon his war in Vietnam," a Citizens for Kennedy pamphlet stated, "or the Democratic Party must abandon Lyndon Johnson." Kennedy believed that, if he challenged Johnson, it would only divide the party, provoke a backlash from the leadership, and be framed in the press as "opportunistic." And it would destroy his chances of winning the presidential nomination in 1972. "You are fond of saying the hottest place in hell is reserved for those who fail to act in times of great moral crisis," the co-chair of Citizens for Kennedy wrote the senator. "With villages burning and men risking their lives daily in this obscene war, I don't think it is asking too much of you to risk your political prestige by becoming an active Presidential candidate."

But Kennedy was too much the party loyalist to break with Johnson. He once again disavowed the Citizens for Kennedy groups and flatly rejected Lowenstein's call for him to lead the Dump Johnson movement. Lowenstein told him he was making a big mistake. Peace Democrats believed Kennedy's increasingly moralistic critique of the war was incompatible with his endorsement of the war's chief perpetrator. The anti-war movement pressed Kennedy to take a stand consistent with his conscience; the Johnson forces demanded absolute loyalty. By the end of 1967, the Vietnam War had claimed nearly 13,000 American lives, and Johnson's rhetoric about "winning" had lost credibility. Yet Kennedy refused to break with his party's leadership.

In November 1967, Minnesota Senator Eugene McCarthy, who served on the Foreign Relations Committee and had been a reliable critic of the war, accepted Lowenstein's challenge to run as a peace candidate in the primaries. The soft-spoken, professorial McCarthy had the reputation of being one of the Senate's most thoughtful opponents of the war. The son of Irish and German immigrants, McCarthy's contemplative demeanor seemed a good palliative for the intense passions of the time. Kennedy's friend and colleague South Dakota Senator George McGovern, who knew both men well, said that Kennedy became "terribly distressed" at the news of McCarthy's entry into the race. He could foresee the political problems McCarthy's candidacy would cause for him. Although McCarthy had far less to lose politically (he admitted that his presidential bid was a symbolic gesture), he had displayed greater courage than Kennedy in agreeing to lead the Dump Johnson effort. With Lowenstein's help, McCarthy tapped into a vast contingent of college students and volunteers who were willing to work long hours for his campaign.

After McCarthy entered the primaries, the Washington press corps was abuzz with speculation about Kennedy's intentions. The press pelted him with questions about whether he would jump into the race if McCarthy exposed Johnson's vulnerability. Publicly, Kennedy welcomed McCarthy's intraparty competition: "There would at least be a discussion," he said, "and one was desperately needed since there had been no real dialogue about Vietnam." Activists asked Kennedy to endorse McCarthy, but he refused to do so. He believed it would only enrage Johnson, and when McCarthy inevitably lost, it would be seen as his defeat as well. His stance seemed calculating and cowardly, and it reinforced among activists the impression of Kennedy as being an "opportunist."

But the political reality that confronted Kennedy was fundamentally different than the one that faced McCarthy. The assassination of President Kennedy had thrust Robert Kennedy into a strange role in the nation's politics. Speculation among Democrats and in the press ran high about his potential to reclaim the throne on behalf of his fallen brother. Whereas McCarthy could afford a chimerical attempt to topple Johnson, Kennedy refused to throw away the political capital he had built up from the earliest days of his brother's career in a futile endeavor to unseat an incumbent President from his own party. Kennedy would never run for President to make a symbolic statement, no matter how strongly he felt about the war. He would run only if he had a chance of winning.

McCarthy campaigned hard throughout New Hampshire, preparing for the first primary election to be held on March 12, 1968. Many of his idealistic young supporters had gone "Clean for Gene," getting haircuts, shaving, and wearing nice clothes to better appeal to the state's conservative voters as they knocked on doors in the freezing winter. Kennedy's office sent out mailings to his allies in New Hampshire, asking them to halt their signature-gathering campaign to place his name on the ballot.

Kennedy told journalists in Washington that, although he believed the Vietnam War was "one of the greatest disasters of all time for the United States," he still would not take on Johnson "under any conceivable circumstances." Later, Kennedy's press secretary, Frank Mankiewicz, prevailed on him to send out a press release changing the word "conceivable" to "foreseeable." Mainstream political commentators, including editorialists from *The New York Times* and *The Washington Post*, were elated that Kennedy had placed "prudence" over "passion" in distancing himself from the peace wing of his party. They praised Kennedy for choosing to remain loyal to his President.

9

Presidential Candidate

On the morning of January 31, 1968, Robert Kennedy attended an off-the-record National Press Club breakfast in Washington, D.C. At the meeting, a journalist tore a copy of a UPI story from a teletype machine and handed it to Kennedy. It was an early report of a massive enemy offensive that had broken out in South Vietnam. Kennedy quickly skimmed the piece and muttered sarcastically: "Yeah, we're winning." Although he didn't know it at the time, the news flash he held in his hands signaled the start of a chain of events that would lead to his final break with Johnson and his own presidential bid.

In Vietnam, on the evening of the Tet lunar new year, amidst the sounds of parades and fireworks, guerrilla fighters of the National Liberation Front blasted a hole in the concrete wall of the American embassy in Saigon and stormed in with high-caliber machine guns and thousands of rounds of ammunition. They cut the embassy's phone lines, killed six American Military Police (MP) officers, and battered down the doors of the main building. They pinned down American Marines and MPs for seven hours with automatic weapons fire and rocket-propelled grenades. The Tet Offensive included not only the seizure of the American embassy but also thousands of simultaneous assaults in Saigon and every other major city throughout the country.

The U.S.-backed president of South Vietnam, General Nguyen Van Thieu, declared martial law, and General William Westmoreland, the commander of all U.S. forces in Vietnam, ordered the retaking of the U.S. embassy the top priority. When the battle was over, American troops discovered that two MPs had been shot in the back of the head, indicating there had been collaborators inside the compound.

The Tet Offensive had a transformative effect on the public's perception of the war. The fighting in Saigon, Hue, and other cities provided an endless supply of violent and heartrending visuals that Americans watched on the evening news. For weeks, American troops and their South Vietnamese counterparts raced around the country suppressing uprisings. In Saigon, NLF fighters had also seized the nation's largest radio station and blew it to bits in a suicide mission. Others fired mortars that chewed up the tarmacs of the Tan Son Nhut and Bien Hoa Airports. They also hit the Presidential Palace, the South Vietnamese Navy headquarters, a dozen secret police stations, and General Westmoreland's office building.

For years, the Johnson administration had been reassuring the American people that the war in Vietnam was going well. A month before Tet, Johnson declared that the enemy had "met his master in the field." In November 1967, Defense Secretary Robert McNamara, who remained good friends with Robert Kennedy, testified to Congress that the United States was making great progress in winning the "hearts and minds" of the Vietnamese people. The Tet attacks shocked most Americans because they came after years of optimistic rhetoric. The fact that an assault of the size and magnitude of Tet was possible at all belied the administration's claims the United States was "winning." The Tet Offensive set in motion the unraveling of the bipartisan coalition that had backed the war from the start.

In response to the Tet Offensive, the U.S. and South Vietnamese militaries launched an aggressive counterattack, the "post-Tet accelerated pacification program," to hunt down the NLF fighters who had exposed themselves. President Johnson and General Thieu deemed the offensive a "failure" because there had not been a "general uprising" to overthrow the Saigon government. Kennedy followed these events closely while he formulated his response. "Johnson can't get away with saying it was really a victory for us," he told his speechwriter Adam Walinsky. He chose to give a major new address on Vietnam at a previously scheduled book-and-author luncheon in Chicago.

The setting for Kennedy's first comprehensive statement on Vietnam since his March 2, 1967, "Stop the Bombing" speech had clear political overtones. Chicago would host the 1968 Democratic National Convention, and Kennedy spoke with Mayor Richard Daley by his side. Daley's power within the Democratic Party far exceeded the Chicago city limits, given his ability to control the Illinois delegation and to set the schedule of speakers at the upcoming convention in August. Daley was a pragmatist, and the Democratic districts in Illinois mattered to him far more than an experiment in "nation building" in Southeast Asia. The death of a friend's son in Vietnam also affected him. Mayor Daley's political base consisted of largely working-class Catholics of diverse ethnic backgrounds, and it mirrored Kennedy's core base in Boston and New York. The Irish Catholic mayor had been a good friend of Joseph P. Kennedy, and the Kennedy family owned an important piece of real estate in Chicago: the enormous Merchandise Mart. Kennedy knew that, if he was to make a realistic effort to unseat Johnson in 1968, he would need Daley on his side.

On February 8, 1968, with Daley's presence sending a clear signal to the Johnson wing of the party, Kennedy set forth a devastating critique of the Vietnam War. The speech marked his final break with the President. It went far beyond his "Stop the Bombing" speech and zeroed in on the central "illusions" of the war. He rejected the putative monopoly on "patriotism" in wartime that the Johnson White House used to discipline its critics.

"Our enemy savagely striking at will across all of South Vietnam," Kennedy began, "has finally shattered the mask of official illusion with which we have concealed our true circumstances, even from ourselves." He refused to accept the Johnson administration's argument that the NLF's failure to overthrow the Saigon government constituted a military "victory" for the United States. "This is not so," he said. The thousands of Vietnamese who conspired to launch the offensive showed that the administration had "misconceived the nature of the war." The war, he said, depended on the "will and the conviction of the Vietnamese people," and the United States could not "win a war that the South Vietnamese cannot win for themselves." Kennedy tore away the web of official lies that claimed the United States was winning: "We have an ally in name only. We support a government without supporters. Without the efforts of American arms that government would not last a day."

He questioned the pursuit of a military victory in Vietnam no matter what the cost: "For the people of Vietnam the last three years have meant little but horror." The small nation had been "devastated by a weight of bombs and shells greater than Nazi Germany knew in the Second World War," and "whole provinces have been substantially destroyed." He rejected the notion that "the American national interest is identical with—or should be subordinated to—the selfish interest of an incompetent military regime."

"With all the lives and resources we have poured into Vietnam," he continued, "is there anyone to argue that a government with any support from its people, with any competence to rule, with any determination to defend itself, would not long ago have been victorious over any insurgent movement, however assisted from outside its borders?" Given the military stalemate and the ineptitude of the Thieu regime, Kennedy believed there was no choice but to negotiate a final settlement and withdraw American forces. His most revealing statement came in the form of yet another mea culpa:

> For twenty years, first the French and then the United States, have been predicting victory in Vietnam. In 1961 and 1962, as well as 1966 and 1967, we have been told that "the tide is turning"; there is "light at the end of the tunnel," "we can soon bring home the troops—victory is near—the enemy is tiring." Once, in 1962, I participated in such predictions myself. But for twenty years we have been wrong. The history of conflict among nations does not record another such lengthy and consistent chronicle of error. It is time to discard so proven a fallacy and face the reality that a military victory is not in sight, and that it probably will never come.

He closed with a final call for deescalating the conflict and expressed his deep concern for the lives of the American troops: "The best way to save our most precious stake in Vietnam—the lives of our soldiers—is to stop the enlargement of the war," and "the best way to end the casualties is to end the war."

Even though nine days earlier Kennedy had publicly endorsed the Democratic ticket, his February 8, 1968, statement made it clear he could not support Johnson's reelection. Excerpts of Kennedy's speech appeared in the major newspapers juxtaposed with reports of continuing NLF attacks. Political writer Tom Wicker offered a sympathetic front-page analysis of the speech in *The New York Times*. Kennedy's place in American politics made it difficult for the pro-war forces to dismiss his analysis. And a peace candidate was already challenging Johnson in the primaries and galvanizing support.

Kennedy's Chicago speech was a timely rebuttal to the administration's attempts to portray Tet as an American victory. He had cleared the way for other commentators and politicians to take stronger stands. Nineteen days after Kennedy spoke in Chicago, CBS News anchorman Walter Cronkite reached the same conclusion. In a special report to an audience of millions, he said: "[T]he only rational way out . . . will be to negotiate, not as victors, but as honorable people who lived up to their pledge to defend democracy, and did the best they could." After watching Cronkite that evening, President Johnson believed he had lost the American middle class on the war.

On the day the Tet Offensive broke out, a 19-second incident on a Saigon street exposed the American people to the true nature of the war. Television viewers were horrified when they watched General Nguyen Ngoc Loan, the chief of South Vietnam's national police, remove his snub-nosed revolver from its holster, place it to the temple of a bound NLF suspect, and pull the trigger. An NBC News crew filmed the macabre spectacle, and an American photojournalist won a Pulitzer Prize for capturing the grisly scene. The images of the pro-U.S. general coolly executing a prisoner of war (POW), wrote journalist Charles Kaiser, "probably did more damage to the idea that America was bringing civilization to South Vietnam than any other event."

The Johnson administration claimed that General Loan had shot the suspect "in the heat of battle" and that "summary executions" of enemy soldiers dressed in civilian clothes were justified. A worried wife of an American POW saw things differently; she sent a telegram to Robert Kennedy: "How can the United States allow public executions of the Vietcong?" she asked. "My husband is a prisoner of war in North Vietnam and I am concerned for his treatment. What has happened to Americans? Do we no longer value the ideals that my brother died for in World War Two and we thought my husband fought for in this war?" Kennedy spoke about the incident in his Chicago speech:

> Last week a Vietcong suspect was turned over to the Chief of the Vietnamese Security Services, who executed him on the spot—a flat violation of the Geneva Convention on the Rules of War. Of course, the enemy is brutal and cruel, and has done the same thing many times. But we are not fighting the Communists in order to become more like them—we fight to preserve our differences. . . . The photograph of the execution was on front pages all around the world—leading our best and oldest friends to ask, more in sorrow than in anger, what has happened to America?

Kennedy's interpretation of the Loan execution was more in accord with the mood of the country than were the administration's attempts to marginalize the event.

Tet pushed public opinion in the direction of the peace movement. Senator McCarthy's challenge took on new relevance, and Kennedy's office was bombarded with letters and telegrams demanding that he run for President. The Congress also grew uneasy. Representatives noticed a dramatic shift in opinion as mail flooded in, calling on them to bring the troops home. Johnson and the pro-war leadership argued that, since all of the cities had been recaptured, Tet was in reality a military success for the United States. "How ironic it is," Kennedy noted wryly, "that we should claim a victory because a people whom we have given sixteen thousand lives, billions of dollars and almost a decade to defend, did not rise in arms against us."

By the spring of 1968, President Johnson was on the defensive despite his legislative accomplishments and landslide victory in 1964. On March 12, 1968, when New Hampshire voters went to the polls, McCarthy fared far better than anyone had predicted, winning 42 percent of the vote to Johnson's 49 percent. It was a historic showing for a candidate who challenged an incumbent President, and it laid bare Johnson's vulnerability. It also added to the "unforeseeable" circumstances needed for Kennedy to reevaluate his own decision to stay out of the race. On the night of the primary election, television news reporter Dan Rather asked the question: "Will Gene McCarthy's showing be enough to tempt Kennedy into an open race for the Democratic nomination?" He then quoted a close friend of President Johnson who said: "We just don't know what Bobby will do, but McCarthy and New Hampshire don't mean a thing unless they mean Bobby is coming in."

On March 12, Kennedy spent the day in Delano, California, attending a Catholic service with César Chávez and several hundred UFW members. Chávez had fasted for 25 days in a symbolic act to urge his more militant followers to commit themselves to nonviolence. In the sweltering Central Valley sun, Kennedy sat next to Chávez, who was severely weakened from the fast, and broke bread with him. During Kennedy's visit, Chávez and others from the UFW sensed that Kennedy was seriously considering entering the presidential race.

The next day, in a letter to his friend, journalist Anthony Lewis, Kennedy wrote in his scrunched, almost illegible handwriting: "The country is in such difficulty, and I believe headed for even more that it almost fills one with despair."

> I just don't know what Johnson is thinking. But when I realize all of that I wonder what I should be doing. But everyone I respect with the exception of Dick Goodwin and Arthur Schlesinger have been against my running. My basic inclination and reaction was to try, and let the future take care of itself. However the prophecies of future doom if I took this course

Kennedy breaking bread on March 12, 1968, with César Chávez, co-founder of the UFW who had fasted for 25 days in the name of nonviolence. A strong friendship was forged between the two leaders. *Photo Credit*: John F. Kennedy Library

made to me by Bob McNamara and to a lesser extent Bill Moyers plus the politicians' almost unanimously feeling that my running would bring about the election of Richard Nixon and many other Republican rightwingers because I would so divide and split the party, and that I could not possibly win—all this made me hesitant—I suppose even more than that.

But the last two days have seen [Secretary of State Dean] Rusk before the Foreign Relations Committee, the New Hampshire primary—and in the last week it has been quite clear that Johnson is also going to do nothing about the riot panel.

So once again—what should I do.
By the time you read this letter both of us will know. . . .

Two days later Kennedy's period of indecision ended. On the evening of March 15, he sent out a mass telegram to Democratic politicians, notifying them that he planned to challenge Johnson for the nomination. He also dispatched Edward Kennedy and Richard Goodwin to Wisconsin, the location of the next primary, to inform Senator McCarthy of his decision. McCarthy, according to Goodwin, who had worked for him, greeted the news of Kennedy entering the race with an outward display of indifference. He appreciated the gesture of letting him know, but he would follow his own course.

The next morning Kennedy entered the Corinthian-columned Senate Caucus Room with Ethel and nine of their ten children. He stood in the same spot where in 1960 John F. Kennedy, also at the age of 42, announced his bid for the presidency and opened with the identical words his brother had used: "I am announcing today my candidacy for the presidency of the United States." It was the place where RFK had begun his career as a young counsel grilling witnesses for the McClellan Committee. The reconciliation between races and classes in America and the ending of the war would be the dominant themes of his campaign. "I run for the presidency because I want the Democratic Party and the United States of America to stand for hope instead of despair," he said. "I do not lightly dismiss the dangers and the difficulties of challenging an incumbent President. But these are not ordinary times and this is not an ordinary election. At stake is not simply the leadership of our party and even our country. It is our right to moral leadership of this planet." *Time* magazine called Kennedy's entrance into the race "the most explosive situation in decades."

At a press conference right after his announcement, Kennedy faced a barrage of questions from Washington journalists. They demanded he respond to the charges of "opportunism" that arose after he jumped into the race so soon after McCarthy's impressive showing in New Hampshire. And they asked him why he was dividing the Democratic Party. "I think the New Hampshire primary established that the division exists in this country, the divisions that exist in the Democratic Party are there, that I haven't brought that about." But little he said could mollify those who questioned his motives. "I am not asking for a free ride," he finally blurted out. "I have got five months ahead of me as far as the convention is concerned. I am going to go into the primaries. I am going to present my case to the American people. I am going to go all across this country. I believe in that system of going in and having one's self tested before the American people. I am willing to do that. The people will be the judge."

Kennedy had missed the New Hampshire primary and the deadline to register for Wisconsin. The next election was in Indiana, and some of his advisers told him to pass on it because they believed it was too risky. He overrode their concerns, saying that "the whole campaign is a gamble" and that he needed to compete for as many delegates as possible. The other primaries he could still enter were in Nebraska, the District of Columbia, Oregon, South Dakota, California, and New York. Kennedy knew it was a long shot, but those around him sensed an enormous load had been lifted from his shoulders. Now that his thoughts and actions were once again in alignment, he began the political battle of his life. Ethel, who had been urging him to run all along, was elated, and so were the younger members of his staff.

Kennedy recruited the old hands from his brother's past campaigns, such as Larry O'Brien, Kenny O'Donnell, Theodore Sorensen, and Jerry Bruno, who had been John Kennedy's "advance man." He fused this group with his Senate staff, which included the political veterans Frederick Dutton and Joseph Dolan and the younger idealists Adam Walinsky, Peter Edelman, and Richard Goodwin. The challenge centered on how to beat McCarthy in the remaining primaries and use the victories to press Democrats nationally for support.

From the beginning of Kennedy's 1968 presidential campaign, the atmosphere was frenetic. He dashed all over the country, to primary and nonprimary states alike, speaking to large, often unruly crowds. He pursued a countrywide strategy that he hoped would culminate in a floor fight at the Democratic National Convention in Chicago, scheduled for August 26. The Johnson Democrats were furious. They predicted that Kennedy would split the party and make it easier for the likely Republican candidate, Richard Nixon, to win. McCarthy supporters saw Kennedy as a usurper who did not have the courage to enter the race until their candidate unmasked Johnson's weakness. They called him "Bobby Come Lately."

On March 18, 1968, two days after Kennedy's announcement, he found himself speaking to students at Kansas State University (KSU) at an event that had been scheduled before he became a candidate. He gave the spirited crowd of 14,000 young people an emotional speech. Although he regretfully admitted that he was "involved in many of the early decisions of Vietnam, decisions which helped set us on our present path," he singled out President Johnson as being responsible for the disaster in Southeast Asia. Johnson's Vietnam policies were "bankrupt," he said, and "deeply wrong." "I am concerned that at the end of it all there will only be more Americans killed; more of our treasure spilled out; and because of the bitterness and hatred on every side in this war, more hundreds of thousands of

Vietnamese slaughtered; so that they may say, as Tacitus said of Rome: 'They made a desert, and called it peace.'"

He quoted the American Army captain who told reporters, after wiping out the village of Ben Tre, that it had been "necessary to destroy the village in order to save it." "Where does such logic end?" Kennedy asked. "If it becomes 'necessary' to destroy all of South Vietnam in order to 'save' it, will we do that too? And if we care so little about South Vietnam that we are willing to see the land destroyed and its people dead, then why are we there in the first place? Can we ordain to ourselves the awful majesty of God to decide what cities and villages are to be destroyed, who will live and who will die, and who will join the refugees wandering in a desert of our own creation?" Kennedy closed his speech to thunderous applause: "So I come here today to ask your help: not for me, but for your country and for the people of Vietnam. . . . I ask you, as tens of thousands of young men and women are doing all over this land, to organize yourselves, and then to go forth and work for new policies, work to change our direction."

Kennedy also spoke that day at the more affluent University of Kansas, where he graphically described the conditions of the urban poor and challenged students to dedicate themselves to working to eradicate poverty in America. The University of Kansas had a total of 16,000 students, but over 20,000 showed up to hear Kennedy speak at the Phineas Allen Fieldhouse; as had been the case at KSU, Kennedy's crowds were the largest in campus history. "We've dropped more bombs on North Vietnam and South Vietnam than we dropped on Germany during the whole Second World War," he said. "What else can you bomb? Who else can you kill? The commander at Ben Tre said he had to destroy the village in order to save it—38,000 people—I'm not blaming him. But I'm blaming me. And I'm blaming you. We are the American people and we permitted that."

On March 21, 1968, Kennedy traveled to Georgia, Alabama, and Tennessee in one day. At the University of Alabama, where nearly five years earlier Governor George Wallace had stood in the schoolhouse door to block Kennedy's efforts as attorney general to racially integrate the campus, Kennedy received a surprisingly warm welcome from 9,000 students, faculty, and administrators. "I have come here because I seek to join with you in building a better country and a united country. And I come to Alabama because I need your help," he said. "This election will mean nothing if it leaves us, after it is all over, as divided as we were when it began. We have to begin to put our country together again. So I believe that any who seek high office this year must go before all Americans: Not just those who agree with them, but also those who disagree; recognizing that it is not just our supporters, not just those who vote for us, but all Americans, who we must lead in the difficult years ahead. And this is why I have come, at the outset of my campaign, not to New York or Chicago or Boston, but here to Alabama."

At Vanderbilt University in Nashville, Kennedy launched into a powerful disquisition on the meaning of dissent in America, which became a frequent campaign theme. He quoted French existentialist philosopher Albert Camus: "I should like to be able to love my country and still love justice." And he defended those who were calling for fundamental change in America, saying they were not the ones responsible for dividing the country.

Kennedy then set off for California, where he visited the cities of Stockton, Sacramento, San Jose, Monterey, and Los Angeles. Robert Donovan of the *Los Angeles Times* reported: "If the spectacle of the first nine days suggests anything, it is that the Kennedy candidacy has touched a live nerve. The people are troubled by war and racial tension. Especially in California, the reaction of the crowds was an indication that the Kennedy candidacy offered them some vague new hope." Kennedy then visited eight states in rapid succession, only one of them a primary state. An article in the March 25 *Los Angeles Times* summarized: "Kennedy's main objective is to stir up such tremendous excitement with an unprecedented springtime nationwide campaign that the shockwaves will jar loose Democratic delegates now aligned with the President."

The Kennedy campaign quickly tapped into a vast reservoir of activists from Citizens for Kennedy, the UFW, the "Mobe," and student and civil rights groups. Strategically, the campaign sought to mobilize at the grass roots, win delegates, and impress the party bosses who would ultimately decide the nominee. The trick was to convince the party elders that Kennedy was the only candidate who could win for the Democrats in November. Kennedy found himself at the center of a struggle for the soul of the Democratic Party.

On March 30, while addressing an outdoor rally at a Phoenix shopping mall, Kennedy spoke of the country's youth being sacrificed needlessly in Vietnam: "As we stand here today, brave young men are fighting across an ocean," he said. "Here, while the sun shines, men are dying on the other side of the earth. Which of them might have written a great symphony? Which of them might have cured cancer? Which of them might have played in a World Series or given us the gift of laughter from a stage or helped build a bridge or a university? Which of them would have taught a child to read?" He implored President Johnson to stop sending young men to die because of his "empty vanities," and he called for bringing the troops "back into American life."

In the wake of the Tet Offensive, Johnson convened a prestigious group of current and former military and foreign policy experts to analyze the situation in Vietnam and to make suggestions. Called the Senior Advisory Group, or the "Wise Men," the committee had met once before, in November 1967, when it recommended staying the course. Johnson expected the "Wise Men" to once again offer their imprimatur for his war policies, but he was astonished to learn that the majority of them had changed their minds after Tet. They now recommended deescalation. Johnson demanded to hear the same briefings from the Joint Chiefs and the CIA that the committee had received. General Westmoreland's secret request to send 206,000 additional troops, which was leaked to the press, marked the tipping point. Meeting on March 25 and 26, the "Wise Men" could not get straight answers from Pentagon officials. No one in the government could answer basic questions about the interdiction of arms moving south, the strength of the NLF in the countryside, or the reliability of the Army of the Republic of Vietnam.

Johnson faced other problems as well. He had to raise taxes to pay for both the war and his new social programs. The U.S. economy was starting to show signs of strain, and the President was predicted to do poorly in the upcoming Wisconsin primary, scheduled for April 2. Nearly one-third of the House of Representatives sponsored a resolution calling for a congressional review of Southeast Asia policy. And young people chanted outside the White House: "Hey, Hey, LBJ! How Many Kids Did You Kill Today?" The latest Gallup poll gave Johnson his lowest approval rating ever.

On the evening of March 31, 1968, Robert Kennedy was sitting in a commercial airplane on the tarmac of La Guardia Airport in New York City. The chairman of the New York State Democratic Party, John Burns, rushed aboard the aircraft and announced: "The President is not going to run!" Kennedy's response: "You're kidding?" At the end of an address to the nation that evening, President Johnson said he would not accept his party's nomination for another term. It was the latest political bombshell in an election year filled with them. The incumbent President, who had won his last election by nearly 16 million votes, had become so crippled by his failures in Vietnam that he withdrew from the race. Kennedy wondered aloud if Johnson would have stepped down had he not challenged him. Just before midnight that evening, Kennedy sent Johnson a telegram saying, in part, "Your decision regarding the Presidency subordinates self to country and is truly magnanimous." He "earnestly" requested "an opportunity to visit" Johnson "as soon as possible to discuss how we might work together in the interest of national unity during the coming months."

On April 3, 1968, the two men met in the Oval Office. Despite their mutual loathing of each other, the encounter was cordial. Kennedy was deferential to Johnson, who seemed to be in good spirits. He sat patiently while Johnson delivered a monologue that lasted nearly half an hour. At one point, Johnson said he always viewed his presidency as carrying on the legacy of John Kennedy. According to the official notes of the meeting, Robert Kennedy politely inquired if it would be okay to ask Johnson a "political" question. The President nodded, and Kennedy asked him point blank: "Where do you stand in the campaign? Are you opposed to my effort and will you marshal forces against me?" Johnson launched into another soliloquy and then said: "I will tell the Vice President about the same things I'm telling you. I don't know if he will run or not. If he asks my advice, I won't give it." He told Kennedy that he did not consider himself a "kingmaker" and that he planned to "stay out of pre-convention politics." Kennedy shared his hope that they could meet again before he endorsed another candidate. "If I move, you'll know," Johnson said. The two powerful Democrats seemed to have reached a truce.

But after Kennedy left the Oval Office, Johnson called in Vice President Humphrey for an "off the record" meeting during which Johnson advised him to jump into the race right away. Johnson told Humphrey that he needed to focus aggressively on winning the endorsements of the power brokers from six states: New Jersey, Pennsylvania, Illinois, Michigan, Ohio, and Indiana. He said he "did not know how Daley and [New Jersey Governor Richard] Hughes and others would come out." But he told Humphrey that it was "possible that, in the end, Daley and Hughes would go with Kennedy." Although pundits gave Kennedy long odds in his bid to win the nomination, Johnson, the master politician, warned Humphrey he was in for a tough fight.

10

From Victory to Tragedy

On April 4, 1968, Kennedy was on his way to Indianapolis to speak at a campaign rally outside an African-American community center. Before boarding a flight to Muncie, he was informed that a gunman had shot Martin Luther King, Jr., in Memphis, Tennessee. The 39-year-old civil rights leader had taken time out from organizing the Poor People's Campaign to lead a nonviolent march of black garbage collectors who were locked in a bitter strike. When Kennedy's plane landed, he heard the terrible news that Dr. King was dead. A shot from a high-powered rifle had struck him in the neck, and he had bled to death in front of room 306 on the second-floor balcony of the Lorraine Motel.

The news of the killing spread rapidly, and cities across America exploded into rioting. The Republican mayor of Indianapolis, Richard Lugar, as well as the chief of police, warned Kennedy not to go into the black part of town because they expected an uprising. Ignoring them, Kennedy sent Ethel to a hotel and then went to speak to a crowd of about 4,000 people; most of those present had not yet heard of King's fate. He skipped being introduced and climbed onto a flatbed truck that served as a makeshift stage. It was a drizzly night with gusty winds, and a lone floodlight barely illuminated the platform. Standing in front of a bulky microphone, Kennedy spoke extemporaneously:

> Ladies and Gentlemen, I am only going to talk to you just for a minute or so this evening because I have some very sad news for all of you. I have bad news for you, for all of our fellow citizens, and people who love peace all over the world, and that is that Martin Luther King was shot and killed tonight.

Those gathered let out an audible gasp, followed by shouts of "No!" Kennedy paused for a moment, and then continued:

> Martin Luther King dedicated his life to love and to justice for his fellow human beings, and he died because of that effort.
>
> In this difficult day, in this difficult time for the United States, it is perhaps well to ask what kind of a nation we are and what direction we want to move in. For those of you who are black—considering the evidence there evidently is that there were white people who were responsible—you can be filled with bitterness, with hatred, and a desire for revenge. We can move in that direction as a country, in great polarization—black people amongst black, white people amongst white, filled with hatred for one another.
>
> Or we can make an effort, as Martin Luther King did, to understand and to comprehend, and to replace that violence, that stain of bloodshed that has spread across our land, with an effort to understand with compassion and love.
>
> For those of you who are black and tempted to be filled with hatred and distrust at the injustice of such an act, against all white people, I can only say that I feel in my own heart the same kind of feeling. I had a member of my family killed, but he was killed by a white man. But we have to make an effort in the United States, we have to make an effort to understand, to go beyond these rather difficult times.
>
> My favorite poet was Aeschylus. He wrote: 'In our sleep, pain which cannot forget falls drop by drop upon the heart until, in our own despair, against our will, comes wisdom through the awful grace of God.'
>
> What we need in the United States is not division; what we need in the United States is not hatred; what we need in the United States is not violence or lawlessness; but love and wisdom, and compassion toward one another, and a feeling of justice toward those who still suffer within our country, whether they be white or they be black. . . .
>
> We've had difficult times in the past. We will have difficult times in the future. It is not the end of violence; it is not the end of lawlessness; it is not the end of disorder.
>
> But the vast majority of white people and the vast majority of black people in this country want to live together, want to improve the quality of our life, and want justice for all human beings who abide in our land.

>Let us dedicate ourselves to what the Greeks wrote so many years ago: to tame the savageness of man and to make gentle the life of the world.

>Let us dedicate ourselves to that, and say a prayer for our country and for our people.

It was the only time Kennedy spoke publicly about his brother's murder. That night violence engulfed 110 cities and caused 39 deaths and 2,500 injuries. Parts of Washington, D.C., were on fire, and the Army deployed machine gunners on the roof of the Capitol. But Indianapolis stayed calm that night. Kennedy sent members of his staff to assist Coretta Scott King, and he quietly had a plane chartered to carry King's body back to Atlanta. He suspended all campaign activities.

The next day African-American community leaders in Cleveland urged Kennedy not to cancel a previously scheduled speaking engagement, and he used the opportunity to condemn the violence in America: "What has violence ever accomplished?" he asked. "We calmly accept newspaper reports of civilian slaughter in far off lands. We glorify killing on movie and television screens and call it entertainment. [And] we make it easy for men of all shades of sanity to acquire whatever weapons and ammunition they desire." Yet violence, Kennedy said, went beyond the use of guns: "For there is another kind of violence, slower but just as deadly destructive as the shot or the bomb in the night. This is the violence of institutions; indifference and inaction and slow decay. This is the violence that afflicts the poor, that poisons relations between men because their skin has different colors. This is the slow destruction of a child by hunger, and schools without books and homes without heat in the winter."

On April 9, Kennedy attended King's funeral at the Ebenezer Baptist Church, where King's father and grandfather had begun their ministries. President Johnson, Hubert Humphrey, Eugene McCarthy, and other national figures were also present. Some of King's closest colleagues, including John Lewis, who would become a congressional representative, and Andrew Young, who later served as ambassador to the United Nations, felt a new appreciation for Kennedy as they walked alongside the old mule wagon that carried King's casket to the cemetery. Young said that King had "admired Bobby's blend of 'crusader' and realistic politician," and he recalled that King had "always placed a great deal of hope in the fact that Bobby was a force to be reckoned with, and stood in the wings as a 'beacon of hope' for the poor, the black, the young and the otherwise alienated idealists of our nation." Kennedy had come a long way since his days as attorney general, when he granted the FBI permission to wiretap King.

The killing of Martin Luther King, Jr., was a staggering blow to the civil rights movement. Organizing the Poor People's Campaign was far more difficult now. Kennedy's presidential campaign and King's mobilization of the poor had been moving along parallel tracks. A large outpouring from African-American voters was essential if Kennedy were to win the Democratic primaries. King's death had a devastating effect on the black electorate, and Kennedy had lost an informal ally. Still he pushed on with his campaign and continued to echo many of the central themes of the poor people's movement: "In my judgment it is imperative that we lessen the gulf which divides those who have, and those who do not," Kennedy said. "I do not believe our nation can survive unless we are able to accomplish a change which brings with it an acceptable way of life for all. If one segment of our society is impoverished, it impoverishes us all."

In Indiana, the Democratic Party machine backed Governor Roger Branigan, who defended Johnson's Vietnam policies. McCarthy was on the ballot, but he had focused most of his attention on Wisconsin (which he won on April 2 with 56 percent of the vote). Kennedy attracted labor support from the autonomous local unions that bucked their leadership's endorsement of the administration's candidate. United Auto Workers (UAW) President Walter Reuther, who had helped John Kennedy in 1960, urged the UAW locals in Indiana to remain neutral. Most observers believed Reuther would endorse Kennedy after he won a few primaries.

Indiana was a tough state for a New York City liberal. Support for the Vietnam War ran high among Hoosiers, and right-wing Republicans owned the major newspapers. In 1964, George Wallace had run an openly racist campaign in the state's primary and garnered nearly a third of the vote. To bypass the Democratic Party leadership, the Kennedy campaign tried to create a groundswell of multiracial support. Toward this end, the candidate embarked on a traditional "whistle-stop" train tour of rural Indiana, while continuing to build Kennedy organizations in the cities. The train, nicknamed "the Wabash Cannon Ball," stopped in dozens of rustic little towns to challenge Governor Branigan in the countryside, where he was assumed to be more popular than Kennedy.

The campaign spent long hours registering voters in the African-American and working-class precincts of Indiana's urban centers, including Gary, where a year earlier Richard Hatcher had become the city's first black mayor. The cities of Lake County bordered Mayor Daley's Chicago, and Daley could not ignore the enthusiasm Kennedy generated. The campaign reached out to the working-class ethnic enclaves by holding numerous campaign events and saturating their newspapers and radio stations. "There has to be a new kind of coalition," Kennedy told journalist Jack Newfield in Indiana, "to keep the Democratic Party going, and to keep the country together.... We have to write off the unions and the South now, and replace them with Negroes, blue-collar whites, and the kids." Common economic conditions would be the tie that bound. "We have to convince the Negroes and poor whites that they have common interests. If we can reconcile those two hostile groups, and then add the kids, you can really turn this country around."

On the final day of the Indiana campaign, Kennedy rode in an eight-hour motorcade sandwiched between Mayor Hatcher and Tony Zale, a former middleweight boxing champion who was a hero in the blue-collar neighborhoods. The three of them symbolized the coalition of working-class whites and African Americans that Kennedy hoped to forge.

On May 7, 1968, Kennedy won the Indiana primary with 42 percent of the vote to Branigan's 31 percent. (McCarthy garnered 27 percent.) Nine out of ten African-American precincts voted for Kennedy, and he even won a few of the "backlash" districts that had voted for George Wallace in 1964. The District of Columbia also held its primary that day, and Kennedy beat the slate backing Humphrey 63 percent to 38 percent. The African-American vote was pivotal in both races. With the two victories, Kennedy won 86 delegates. But he still had a long way to go; to win the nomination, a candidate needed 1,312 delegate votes. The goal of the campaign was to lock down as many delegates as possible to block any candidate from winning the nomination on the first ballot at the convention. Only then could Kennedy negotiate with Daley and the other power brokers to eke out a win. It was a gamble, but in Indiana, Kennedy showed the party regulars he could energize the Democratic base.

Indiana was a conservative state, but Kennedy felt he had connected with the people: "I like Indiana," he confided to Newfield. "The people were fair to me. They gave me a chance. They listened to me. I could see this face, way in back in the crowd, and he was listening, really listening to me. The people here are not so neurotic and hypocritical as in Washington or New York. They're more direct. I like rural people, who work hard with their hands. There is something healthy about them. I loved the faces here in Indiana," he said, "on the farmers, on the steelworkers, on the black kids." Kennedy's next contest depended on whether Nebraska voters would be equally magnanimous.

In Nebraska, Kennedy faced many of the same challenges he had in Indiana. Nebraskans were conservative, rural, and suspicious of outsiders. But in Omaha and a few other cities, he had a base among workers and African Americans. Ted Sorensen's brother, Philip, had been the state's lieutenant governor, and in 1966, he had made an unsuccessful bid for governor. He knew the state well and provided the campaign with voter lists and contacts with state officials. As Kennedy had done in Indiana, he toured the state, starting in the urban centers and then fanning out to the agricultural areas.

Since only about 150,000 people would be voting in the primary, the Kennedy forces ran an efficient campaign that targeted nearly every registered voter with direct mail and telephone calls. Humphrey didn't participate, so the Nebraska race was between Kennedy and McCarthy. McCarthy had spent little time in the state, writing in his memoir that "Nebraska happened on the way west." In the town of Beatrice, Kennedy joked that he and Ethel and their "eleven children" might move there. Reporters began scribbling in their notepads because it was the first time the public had learned that Ethel was expecting their eleventh child. (Ethel's most recent arrivals were Matthew Maxwell Taylor Kennedy, who was born in January 1965, and Douglas Harriman Kennedy, who arrived in March 1967. Rory Kennedy would be born that October.) Robert and Ethel were inseparable on the campaign trail, and when they were apart, they were known to speak on the phone as often as 15 times a day. All along Ethel had been a driving force urging him to run; she knew that sitting on the sidelines in such a pivotal year would have taken a terrible toll on him. On election day, Kennedy won 52 percent of the Nebraska vote to McCarthy's 31 percent. He picked up 25 more delegates. Mayor Daley called the win "a very impressive victory," which is exactly what Kennedy wanted.

Kennedy was also on the ballot in South Dakota, where he received the help of Senator George McGovern, who shared his mailing lists and advised the campaign. In mid-April, when Kennedy came to Sioux Falls, McGovern told the crowd that he would make "one of the three or four greatest presidents in our national history." The intense rivalry between Kennedy and McCarthy in Oregon and California overshadowed the South Dakota primary. Kennedy's political counselors told him not to waste valuable time campaigning on South Dakota's Indian reservations. But Kennedy dismissed their advice and toured several Native American communities even though they accounted for very few votes. He was among a handful of senators who spoke out against the poverty, alcoholism, and suicide rates among indigenous peoples, and he chaired the Senate Subcommittee on Indian Education, which he had created. In his speech announcing his candidacy, Kennedy had pointed to the plight of Native Americans, and he was not going to turn his back on them now. Later, when he beat McCarthy in South Dakota 50 percent to 20 percent (with Humphrey earning 30 percent), he excitedly asked reporters: "Did you hear about the Indians?" He was thrilled to hear that one Native American precinct had given Humphrey 9 votes, McCarthy 2, and Kennedy 878.

The Oregon primary proved to be the most difficult of Kennedy's career. Oregon Representative Edith Green, who in 1960 had worked for John Kennedy's campaign, was charged with galvanizing the state's Democrats. But McCarthy had invested a lot of time lining up college students and suburban voters, and he had largely cemented the anti-war vote. In Oregon, the "well-oiled Kennedy machine" that journalists had written about was sputtering and in need of repair. The state had a tiny African-American population and a history of KKK activity. The working-class whites were heavily supportive of Republican views on the social issues of hunting and gun ownership, and the Oregon Teamsters opposed Kennedy for his work on the McClellan Committee, during which he investigated the Portland local for corruption. McCarthy led in the polls, and by the time Kennedy sent in his political miracle workers to try to salvage the situation, it was too late. The state was not amenable to his practice of mobilizing minorities and the disfranchised. There were not many poor people, and the suburbs and college towns belonged to McCarthy. Kennedy respectfully acknowledged McCarthy's supporters; they represented a bloc of voters he would need later if he was to succeed. "The real struggle in 1968," he said in Oregon, "is between those candidates who espouse change and the candidate who stands for the status quo."

On May 21, McCarthy gave a filmed interview during which he responded to a reporter's query about whether his goal was to block Kennedy: "Sometimes the spoiler role is pretty effective. I think I've been more constructive in this campaign than anyone else. You can say that Bobby spoiled it for me by coming in." McCarthy belittled Kennedy: "Bobby threatened to hold his breath unless the people of Oregon voted for him." He even hinted that he might throw his delegates to Humphrey at the convention. Although McCarthy later backtracked, the thought of him helping Humphrey (who was committed to the war) drew harsh criticism from his peace movement volunteers. Several high-profile activists defected from McCarthy to Kennedy.

As the May 28 election approached, Kennedy's poll numbers in Oregon continued to slide, and the press ridiculed him for abruptly fleeing the Portland zoo upon spying McCarthy's arrival. The Oregon result was 39 percent for Kennedy and 45 percent for McCarthy (the Humphrey slate won 12 percent). The Kennedys had been undefeated in 26 elections, and Oregon had broken their winning streak. Representative Green failed to deliver her own district. Kennedy sent a congratulatory telegram to McCarthy, which was a courtesy McCarthy had not bestowed on Kennedy after Indiana and Nebraska.

At the Benson Hotel in Portland, a dejected Kennedy accepted responsibility for the defeat. "Why did I lose? I just didn't do well," he said. He blamed the loss on his inability to connect with Oregon voters. When he was asked how it felt to be the first member of his family to lose after 27 elections, he quoted Abraham Lincoln's joke about the man being run out of town on a rail: "If it wasn't for the honor of the thing—being the first Kennedy to lose—I'd rather have passed it up," he said. He had previously said that his "viability" as a candidate would be in jeopardy if he lost any of the primaries. The defeat was a setback because delegates "will use Oregon as an excuse for not supporting me," he said. Back at his hotel room, a reporter asked him if the loss had hurt him. "It certainly wasn't one of the more helpful developments of the day" was his steely reply.

Yet Kennedy's Oregon loss might have helped him indirectly by energizing his grassroots supporters in California, who realized their candidate was not invincible. César Chávez's UFW and other activists redoubled their efforts as the June 4 primary neared. The pro-Humphrey Democratic leadership hoped that McCarthy might finish off Kennedy in California.

For Kennedy, California was a must-win situation. Despite Republican Ronald Reagan's gubernatorial victory two years earlier, registered Democrats still outnumbered the GOP by over 1 million in a state of 10 million. With its industry and agriculture, the state was a microcosm of the nation. Jesse Unruh, the speaker of the California Assembly, was a Kennedy partisan, but his political organization was unreliable, and Kennedy insiders believed he made decisions based on his own gubernatorial ambitions. Allies of the Johnson administration poured money into the state (some of which allegedly found its way into McCarthy's coffers) and aggressively ran a slate of delegates under the leadership of Thomas Lynch, California's attorney general. As in Oregon, McCarthy's strength could be found largely on the college campuses and in the white suburbs. The Kennedy campaign sought to fuse a coalition of Latinos, African Americans, working-class whites, and middle-class liberals.

On April 28, 1968, Humphrey formally announced his candidacy. He chose not to place his name on the ballot in any of the remaining primaries, and he refused to debate Kennedy and McCarthy. Humphrey had been a New Deal stalwart going back to the Truman administration, and he was a champion of African-American civil rights, labor unions, and progressive social programs. As with Johnson, on the domestic front there was little disagreement between Kennedy and Humphrey. It was the Vietnam War on which they had major differences.

The foot soldiers for Kennedy in California were the hundreds of experienced organizers of the UFW. Chávez and his close associate Dolores Huerta were Kennedy delegates, and they traveled the state speaking at bilingual gatherings. Whenever Chávez heard McCarthy supporters shout: "Where was Kennedy when we were in New Hampshire?" He would reply: "He was walking with me in Delano!" The UFW suspended its strike and grape boycott so its activists could dedicate themselves to helping Kennedy win. "For every one organizer we had who worked for John Kennedy," Chávez said, "we had ten working for Robert Kennedy."

One bilingual campaign pamphlet quoted Chávez: "Senator Kennedy came at a time when our cause was very hard pressed and we were surrounded by powerful enemies who did not hesitate to viciously attack anyone who was courageous enough to help us. He did not stop to ask whether it would be politically wise for him to come . . . nor did he stop to worry about the color of our skin . . . or what languages we speak. . . . We know from our experience that he cares, he understands and he acts with compassion and courage." Kennedy's Irish Catholic roots might have been a detriment with some voters, but with California's overwhelmingly Catholic Latino population, they were an asset. Chávez said that the farm workers looked on Kennedy "as sort of a minority kind of person himself," and therefore "with Senator Kennedy it was like he was ours."

Kennedy's fame and celebrity were also put to use. In 1966, the state had elected a movie actor to be governor, and Kennedy made the most of his plentiful Hollywood contacts. The campaign organized two televised galas, one in the Los Angeles Sports Arena and another in the San Francisco Civic Auditorium, bringing together dozens of famous personalities. Among Kennedy's many entertainment industry supporters were singer Andy Williams (who headed the Hollywood for Kennedy Committee), Peter Lawford (Kennedy's brother-in-law), Richard Burton, Elizabeth Taylor, and Shirley MacLaine. Kennedy's fusing of the wealthy Hollywood elite with Chávez's hard-pressed farm workers transcended the boundaries of race and class. The glitterati active in the campaign also gave the impression that, if Kennedy was elected, he might restore some of the glamour and elegance to the White House that had been missing since his brother's assassination.

In California, Kennedy had the endorsement of the progressive labor movement. The western regional director for the United Auto Workers, Paul Schrade, helped Kennedy peel off union support from the locals despite the American Federation of Labor and Congress of Industrial Organizations' (AFL–CIO) formal endorsement of Humphrey. "Where unions are strong, the cause of progress and social justice is advanced," a Kennedy campaign flyer stated, "and where unions are weak, the whole society suffers." The grassroots labor support for Kennedy showed that he was the candidate of progressive labor unionism.

As the California campaign reached the homestretch, Kennedy picked up his already grueling pace. But he took time off to bring six of his children to Disneyland during the last weekend of the race. On Monday, the final full day of the campaign, Kennedy traversed over 1,200 miles. He went from Los Angeles to San Francisco, back to Long Beach and Watts, and then down to San Diego, reaching all of the state's largest media markets. Everywhere he rode in open motorcades through choked streets, his outstretched arms touching people. His hands were bloodied and scabbed from the thousands of handshakes. Excited fans often removed his cuff links and even his shoes. In San Francisco's Chinatown, firecrackers that sounded like gunfire popped off during the motorcade; Ethel and everyone else in the car ducked instinctively. Thoughts of November 22, 1963, still hovered below the surface. Bedlam followed Kennedy's motorcades, and the candidate, who came from a large, rambunctious family and who lived in a household with ten children and a menagerie of animals, seemed at home amidst the chaos and disorder. He had even brought one of his dogs along with him on the campaign trail.

Kennedy spent the last night before the voting at the Malibu beach house of his friend film director John Frankenheimer. The next morning, on a gray and chilly election day, Kennedy swam in

Kennedy receiving a daisy from a supporter in New York City while on the campaign trail. During his 85-day presidential campaign of 1968, he stepped out from beneath his brother's shadow and became a national leader in his own right. *Photo Credit*: John F. Kennedy Library (Helene Berinsky)

the ocean with a few of his children. David, who was 12, had gotten himself trapped in the undertow. Several tense minutes passed while his father struggled to fish him out. It was a scene reminiscent of the time Kennedy as a young boy leapt into Nantucket Sound, only to be rescued by his big brother Joe.

On June 4, the physical toll of the campaign had caught up with him. Exhausted, he lay sleeping out by Frankenheimer's pool. Richard Goodwin remembered seeing Kennedy "stretched out across two chairs" with "his head hanging limply over the chair frame; his unshaven face deeply lined and his lips slightly parted." Goodwin was relieved to see that his friend was not gravely ill or worse. Later that day the exit polls showed Kennedy leading, and Frankenheimer drove with him to the Ambassador Hotel, the election night headquarters. In the Royal Suite, where a cocktail party was already in full swing, journalists clamored for interviews, but Kennedy waited to watch the returns. The candidate, sensing victory, was relaxed and ebullient in the crammed hotel suite; his mood lightened as he smoked a cigar and joked with friends and family. He told Goodwin, pounding his fist into his palm for emphasis: "My only chance is to chase Hubert's ass all over the country. I'm going to make him debate me!"

Later that night it was clear Kennedy had attained an unsurpassable lead. His enormous showing in the African-American, Latino, and working-class precincts in Los Angeles had sealed his victory. He won with 46 percent of the vote. McCarthy earned an impressive 42 percent and the Humphrey slate, 12 percent. A remarkable piece of voting data indicated that 14 of every 15 Latinos who voted cast their ballots for Kennedy. It had been a close race, but it redeemed Kennedy from his Oregon defeat, and the 170 additional delegates strengthened his hand as the bandwagon continued to roll toward the convention. Before delivering his victory speech, Kennedy telephoned Allard Lownstein in New York, the sight of the next primary on June 18. He wanted Lowenstein to act as a liaison with the McCarthy campaign to help him win over the Minnesotan's delegates now that California established Kennedy as the only viable peace candidate.

At about 11:30 P.M., television news reporters harangued Kennedy to give his speech before Californians retired for the night. Flanked by his aides and half a dozen journalists, he entered a packed elevator and went down to speak. The huge Embassy Ballroom was clogged with celebrants, campaign workers, reporters, photographers, and Kennedy partisans of all kinds. When he finally appeared at the podium, the several thousand revelers greeted him with thunderous applause. "If there is one lesson of this political year," he began, "it is that the people of this country wish to move away from the politics which led to an endless war abroad and to increasing unrest in our own country." Senator McCarthy's supporters "deserve the gratitude of the nation," he said, "for the courageous fight which helped to break the political logjam, demonstrated the desire for change, and helped make citizen participation into a new and powerful force of our political life."

But Kennedy wasted no time in focusing his attention on Humphrey. In all of the primaries, the voters had "rejected those slates of delegates committed to the Johnson-Humphrey Administration," he said. "I cannot believe that the Democratic Party will nominate a man whose ideas and programs have been so decisively rejected. Yet the Vice President apparently believes he can win the nomination without once submitting his case to the people." He wanted a face-to-face meeting: "I will go any place any time to meet the Vice President in a televised debate." Standing at the podium, with Ethel, Jesse Unruh, Dolores Huerta, and many others by his side, Kennedy continued:

> I am the only candidate committed to a realistic negotiated solution to the Vietnamese war, one embracing all the elements of the South Vietnamese population, and opposed to the use of American military force to carry the major burden of what should be essentially a Vietnamese conflict. In fact, I am the only candidate with policies likely to bring an honorable peace to let the killing stop. . . .
>
> What I think is quite clear is that we can work together in the last analysis, and that what has been going on within the United States over a period of the last three years. The divisions, the violence, the disenchantment with our society—the divisions, whether it's between blacks and whites, between the poor and the more affluent, or between age groups, or on the war in Vietnam—is that we can start to work together. We are a great country, an unselfish country and a compassionate country. I intend to make that the basis for running.

He thanked dozens of people by name who were involved in getting out the vote, as well as Ethel, César Chávez, and athletes Rosie Grier and Rafer Johnson, who helped in the black communities. He also thanked his dog "Freckles," who accompanied him on the campaign trail, which evoked cheers and laughter. "Where's Freckles?" someone shouted out; "He's sleeping right now," Kennedy replied with a broad smile. "I thank all of you who made this possible this evening. All the effort you made, and all of the people whose places I haven't been to, but who made or did all of the work at the precinct level, got out the vote . . . brought forth all of the efforts required. I was a campaign manager eight years ago, and I know what a difference that kind of effort, and that kind of commitment can make. My thanks to all of you, and on to Chicago, and let's win there." He flashed a "V" for victory with his right hand, swept back his forelock, and stepped back from the podium.

Amidst a deafening ovation, Kennedy slowly made his way from the dais through the masses of people milling about behind the stage and moved toward a doorway that led to the hotel's kitchen. A press conference was to take place in a room on the other side of the ballroom. Getting there through the kitchen seemed to be wiser than trying to push through the middle of the crowd. He disappeared into the pantry, which was stuffed with some 70 campaign workers, reporters, and food service employees. He paused to shake hands with workers from the hotel staff and to sign a few autographs. Suddenly, a small man to Kennedy's right who had been crouching behind a stack of metal trays lunged forward and began discharging a handgun. A clump of people surged toward the assailant as he wildly emptied his 22-caliber eight-shot revolver. Gunfire wounded five, including union leader Paul Schrade, who was shot in the head. But Kennedy received the worst of it: A single bullet with an upward trajectory had entered his brain from just below his right ear. The muzzle had been no farther than three inches from his head. The gun was a $30 Iver-Johnson pistol.

For 85 days, Kennedy had worked harder and put in longer hours on the campaign than anyone else. He looked forward to a meaningful, relaxing night of celebration. He and Ethel planned to have dinner and drinks with close friends at a swanky Los Angeles eatery. Instead, he found himself collapsed on the greasy concrete floor of the Ambassador Hotel's kitchen pantry.

In the 25 hours following the shooting, Kennedy was transferred to two hospitals, and he underwent 4 hours of brain surgery. As he fought for his life at Good Samaritan Hospital, mournful well-wishers amassed at the front of the building. A makeshift pressroom was set up, and Frank Mankiewicz had the grim task of periodically updating the world about Kennedy's condition. In the end, the damage from bullet and bone fragments was too severe. Mankiewicz made a brief announcement: "Senator Robert Francis Kennedy died at 1:44 A.M. today, June 6, 1968. With the Senator at the time of his death was his wife, Ethel, his sisters, Mrs. Patricia Lawford and Mrs. Stephen Smith, and his sister-in-law, Mrs. John F. Kennedy. He was forty-two years old."

In New York, schools closed, and a television station broadcast the single word "SHAME" for nearly three hours. Ethel Kennedy, who was expecting her eleventh child that October, received over 325,000 letters of sympathy. Condolence telegrams flooded Kennedy's Senate office from Poland, South Africa, Vietnam, Argentina, and dozens of other countries. Sorrow and disbelief produced an "eerie quietness" in the city of Los Angeles. The student editor of the *UCLA Daily Bruin* said he believed the killing of Robert Kennedy would "make young people completely unreachable."

President Johnson responded to the news: "This is a time of tragedy and loss. Senator Robert Kennedy is dead. Robert Kennedy affirmed this country—affirmed the essential decency of its people, their longing for peace, their desire to improve conditions of life for all. . . . Our public life is diminished by his loss." The President ordered Secret Service protection for the remaining candidates and offered the Kennedy family use of Air Force One. Eugene McCarthy suspended his campaign and he linked the tragedy to "the disposition of violence, which we have visited upon the rest of the world."

A Jordanian immigrant was tried, convicted, and sentenced to life in prison for the murder. Press accounts portrayed the 24-year-old Sirhan Bishara Sirhan as a Palestinian extremist. A newspaper clipping found in his pocket reported a speech Kennedy had given to a Los Angeles Jewish group during which he endorsed the sale of jet fighters to Israel. But Kennedy's speech that day was election year boilerplate. The killer had allegedly singled him out because of his mainstream support of the Jewish state.

Although the press portrayed Sirhan as an assassin with a clear political motive, he allegedly filled notebooks with repetitive hand-written gibberish. The phrase "RFK Must Die" is scrawled over and over again, filling pages of his notebooks, followed by "Pay to the Order of" in identical form. They appear to be the work of a psychotic rather than an assassin with "rational" aims. Curious for a fanatic, he never staked claim to his deed but said he could "not remember" the shooting. (It might have been a ploy for his defense to avoid the death penalty.) The mayor of Los Angeles, Sam Yorty, told reporters that Sirhan was a "Communist." The killer's grand "political" motive may have been an afterthought to give meaning to a senseless act in an era plagued by them. Or it may have been an attempt to snuff out public talk of conspiracies after the lingering doubts about the events of November 1963. (A Gallup poll taken the day after Robert Kennedy was shot showed that the public by a wide margin believed it was a product of a conspiracy.) In any case, the historian Philip Melanson and other authors have legitimately questioned some of the actions of the Los Angeles Police Department (particularly Special Unit Senator, which ran the investigation) with respect to the treatment of the crime scene, the interrogation of witnesses, and the handling and destruction of evidence.

Kennedy's body was flown to New York, where he lay for two days in the vaulted nave of St. Patrick's Cathedral. Over 100,000 people lined up for 25 blocks, some of them waiting five or six hours just to walk past his coffin. The diversity of those who came to show their respects was a testimony to Kennedy's wide-ranging appeal. Edward Kennedy gave the eulogy. He had lost the last of his three brothers. He said Robert Kennedy should be remembered "simply as a good and decent man, who saw wrong and tried to right it, saw suffering and tried to heal it, saw war and tried to stop it."

A funeral train carried Kennedy's body to Washington. Thousands of people lined the tracks; some held American flags and plaintively sang "The Battle Hymn of the Republic." On television, as the 20-car train set out on its final leg, with the flag-draped coffin visible in the last car, Walter Cronkite intoned: "It is the end of a brilliant political and public career." Kennedy's death also marked the end of an era and was a grave setback for those who were trying to stop the Vietnam War. On June 8, 1968, he was laid to rest not far from the eternal flame of his brother's grave in Arlington National Cemetery.

Robert Francis Kennedy embodied the roles of activist and politician. His views on the perennial American problems of foreign wars, poverty, and racial strife continue to resonate. He had the unique ability to challenge people morally and to stand together with those who wished to build a more humane society. To many people, RFK's loss marked the death of American idealism because at that time there was no other national leader who could step forward and carry on his quest. He appealed to Americans' highest ideals about democracy and the role of citizen action, while telling them the bitter truth about the Vietnam War and the social injustices in the United States and in the world. The killing of Robert Kennedy was particularly brutal, coming just eight weeks after the assassination of Martin Luther King, Jr., and less than five years after that of President John F. Kennedy. The ideals that the three men shared and their common fate created a lasting association among them in the public mind. But Robert Kennedy's assassination, the last of the three, had the most devastating consequences for the politics of the 1960s. His death came at a time when the nation was bitterly divided, when there were riots in the cities, when there were over half a million American troops in Southeast Asia. The silencing of Robert Kennedy's voice could not have come at a worse time for the nation. He was fond of closing his stump speeches with a quote he held dear from Irish playwright George Bernard Shaw: "Some men see things as they are and say, 'Why?' I dream of things that never were and say, 'Why not?'"

Conclusion

Robert Kennedy's abrupt removal from the nation's political life left in disarray the new Democratic coalition he was working to build. In August 1968, at the Democratic National Convention in Chicago, the consequences of Kennedy's absence played out. The nationally televised street battles in downtown Chicago between peace demonstrators and police spilled onto the convention floor in the form of shoving matches between delegates and had a devastating effect on the party. In 1968, Kennedy was one of the few politicians who could speak the language of the "Old Politics" with machine stalwarts like Chicago Mayor Richard Daley, while still engaging in a constructive dialogue with the anti-war protesters whom Daley's police had beaten outside the convention hall.

Award-winning reporter Theodore White, whose books on *The Making of the President* transformed campaign journalism, privately shared his impressions of the convention with Ethel Kennedy: "I write this from Chicago and the Democratic convention—macabre, unbelievable, grotesque parody on the process of American politics. Most macabre is the spectacle of all our old friends split and divided and squabbling and spitting on each other. It is so goddamned sad. There is no comfort for me in the thought, which I always held, that Bob, had he lived, would have marched through this convention as its master—and then on to the Presidency."

At the close of the convention, the delegates nominated Hubert Humphrey and flatly rejected a "peace plank" the anti-war wing tried to insert into the party's platform. Kennedy's goal at the convention had been to block any candidate from winning the nomination on the first ballot and then aggressively create a stampede effect among delegates toward his camp. His experiences as John Kennedy's standard-bearer at the 1956 and 1960 Democratic conventions gave him an intimate knowledge of the nominating procedures. But it can never be determined whether or not Kennedy would have succeeded. What is known, however, is that Humphrey, who defended the Vietnam War until it proved politically fatal, led a dispirited Democratic Party into the November elections. The grassroots citizen energy that Kennedy and McCarthy had unleashed in the primaries had all but evaporated; there even emerged an anti-Humphrey "Dump the Hump" movement among the youth wing of the party.

The Republican Party's candidate, former Vice President Richard M. Nixon, whom John Kennedy had narrowly defeated in 1960, ran television ads featuring the violence at the Democratic convention. Nixon won the presidency in a close race. And with the exception of President Jimmy Carter's single term, Nixon's 1968 victory ushered in a quarter century of Republican domination of the White House and, along with it, a prolonged identity crisis for the Democrats. Robert Kennedy had said repeatedly that a Nixon presidency would be "unacceptable to the country."

Kennedy, like Martin Luther King, Jr., will be forever identified with the explosion of citizen activism that characterized the 1960s. He had leapt into the rough-and-tumble street politics of 1968, joining with community organizers in small venues and face-to-face meetings. Whether fielding questions in union halls or on college campuses, or getting his hands bloodied in parades and motorcades, Kennedy made an effort to communicate with political activists at the local level, many of whom were far to his left on the political spectrum. The energy of the primary campaigns thrust Kennedy into the center of a volatile grassroots fervor. César Chávez likened the California campaign to "those heated elections they have south of the border." Kennedy took on the task not only because he needed "people power" to succeed but also because by 1968 he largely agreed with the activists' viewpoint.

Kennedy began to look at American society with a far more critical eye. He believed the nation must stand for something other than consumerism and the pursuit of material wealth. "Our Gross National Product now soars above $800 billion a year," he said, "but that counts air pollution and cigarette advertising, and ambulances to clear our streets of carnage. It counts the special locks for our doors and jails for the people who break them. It counts the destruction of our redwoods and the loss of natural wonder to chaotic sprawl. It counts napalm and nuclear warheads and armored cars for the police to fight riots in our cities. It counts Whitman's rifle and Speck's knife, and television programs, which glorify violence to sell toys to our children."

He lamented the loss of a higher purpose for America: "The gross national product does not allow for the health of our children, the quality of their education, or the joy of their play," he said. "It does not include the beauty of our poetry or the strength of our marriages; the intelligence of our public debate or the integrity of our public officials. It measures neither our wit nor our courage; neither our wisdom nor our learning; neither our compassion nor our devotion to our country; it measures everything, in short, except that which makes life worthwhile."

Kennedy's legacy has become contested ground in the decades since his death. Conservatives have embraced his dedication to "law and order" as attorney general and his toughness as a prosecutor. It was Robert Kennedy who put organized crime on notice and who showed his determination by snatching mobster Carlos Marcellos off a New Orleans street and deporting him. He also brought forth Joseph Valachi to blow the whistle on the mafia. Conservatives have also praised Kennedy for his criticisms of Lyndon Johnson's social programs. He believed that the government should not breed dependency but rather provide a safety net while emphasizing self-reliance. His public-private partnership in Bedford-Stuyvesant stands as a model for his goal of creating jobs to help the poor become working taxpayers. Some of Kennedy's working-class supporters were deeply conservative on social issues and, in the years after his death, slowly drifted toward becoming "Reagan Democrats." On November 20, 2001, a Republican administration named the Department of Justice building in honor of Robert F. Kennedy.

In the summer of 1999, President William Jefferson Clinton evoked Robert Kennedy's memory while touring several impoverished communities. He traveled to some of the same places Kennedy had visited in the late 1960s, including the Mississippi Delta and the Pine Ridge Reservation in South Dakota. The President spoke out against the poverty that existed in America and praised Kennedy's daughter Kerry Kennedy for her charitable works. At the same time, Kennedy's former legislative aide Peter Edelman, who served in the Clinton administration, resigned his post in protest after Clinton signed what Edelman believed to be a draconian welfare reform bill. In an op-ed piece in *The New York Times,* Edelman criticized Clinton's expedition, calling it a "cosmetic poverty tour." The episode shows that, even among those who claim to be Robert Kennedy's ideological heirs, the meaning of his legacy is still contested.

Yet there seems to be agreement on all sides that Kennedy was an extremely capable attorney general. He played a pivotal role in dismantling the Jim Crow system of racial segregation in the South, and therefore he should be recognized as one of the most important figures ever to head the Justice Department.

Kennedy's work with César Chávez and the United Farm Workers created a deep and ongoing bond between his family and the struggling Latino agricultural workers. His support for Martin Luther King, Jr.'s Poor People's Campaign and his work on behalf of African-American civil rights have resonated with a younger generation of black political leaders. Currently, the Robert F. Kennedy Memorial Foundation sponsors community projects and has granted cash prizes as part of its yearly human rights award to unsung activists from all over the world who work for social justice.

On November 20, 2005, when the RFK Memorial Foundation sponsored an 80th birthday celebration of Kennedy's life in the nation's capital, noted activists, authors, and politicians spoke about Kennedy's influence on their work. Those who spoke included Senators Edward Kennedy, Barack Obama, Paul Sarbanes, John Kerry, and Hillary Rodham Clinton as well as Representatives Edward Markey, John Lewis, and Dennis Kucinich. Despite having his life cut short, Kennedy's legacy has clearly had a profound and lasting impact on a generation of Democratic leaders.

In his last speech, Kennedy said: "I do not believe I can be successful without your help and support. I ask this, not for myself, but for the cause and the ideas, which moved you to begin this great popular movement. . . . With you I know we can keep faith with the American need and the American desire for peace and for justice, and for a government dedicated to giving the people mastery over their own affairs and future."

Robert Kennedy worked in solidarity with the social movements of the 1960s. He allied himself with farm workers; progressive labor unionists; peace, civil rights, and antipoverty activists; youth; and students. These mobilized citizens, loosely associated with his 1968 campaign, represented a potential for the long-term organized resistance to racism, economic injustice, and jingoistic nationalism. He showed that democracy works best when it is energized from below. Following March 16, 1968, when Kennedy entered the presidential primary races, his 85-day campaign demonstrated a kind of selfless patriotism worthy of emulation. Employing the broad themes of racial solidarity and peace in Vietnam, his campaign became a rallying point for Americans who wished to move the nation in a more egalitarian and compassionate direction. Robert Kennedy's legacy will continue to be contested, but it will be more often than not strongly identified with the spirit of grassroots activism.

Study and Discussion Questions

Chapter 1: Coming of Age

1. What were the main influences on young Robert Kennedy that helped forge his views of American society and politics? What special insights might he have as the child of a family who identified with Irish immigrants?

2. What did young RFK learn from his early encounters with and exposure to the tenets of New Deal liberalism? Explain the general goals and objectives of President Franklin D. Roosevelt's social and political programs. How was FDR's program a direct response to the crisis of the Great Depression? How did the depression affect the Kennedy family?

3. What did you learn from reading this chapter about the brewing tensions in Europe prior to the outbreak of the Second World War? How did the war affect young RFK? How did it affect the Kennedy family?

4. What impact did seeing his two older brothers go off to war have on RFK's worldview?

Chapter 2: Launching a Public Life

1. What lessons did Robert Kennedy learn from working on his brother's congressional and Senate campaigns?

2. What does RFK's work ethic as a college student tell us about his later style of politics? What did he learn about the world while traveling after college? What were the effects of Robert's travels together with his brother John?

3. What do RFK's law school experiences tell us about his evolving views of race relations? Social justice? Liberalism in general?

4. What did RFK learn about politics while managing his brother's 1952 Senate campaign? What did you learn about RFK's abilities as a campaign manager and political organizer?

5. What did you learn about McCarthyism? Why did RFK work for McCarthy's committee? What does McCarthy's meteoric rise in power and final crash tell us about American politics in the 1950s? Were McCarthy's views of the Cold War with the Soviet Union exaggerated or largely correct? What effects did the Army-McCarthy hearings have on the nation's perception of the anti-Communist cause? What happened to McCarthy? Why did RFK choose not to distance himself from the discredited senator?

Chapter 3: Finding His Way in the 1950s

1. What did Robert Kennedy learn about the world when he traveled to the Soviet Union?

2. What were some of the political lessons that RFK learned when he sought the support of Democratic delegates for his brother's vice presidential bid at the 1956 Democratic National Convention? Explain the main problems RFK uncovered concerning Adlai Stevenson's 1956 presidential campaign. Why did RFK vote for Eisenhower?

3. Explain the types of organized criminal activities relating to labor unions that RFK was investigating while he was lead counsel for the McClellan Committee. Why did RFK and James Hoffa lock horns? What were the issues at stake according to RFK? Was RFK successful? Why or why not?

4. How well did RFK manage John Kennedy's 1960 primary campaigns? Why was the issue of John Kennedy's Catholicism such a thorny point of contention during the 1960 primary races?

Chapter 4: His Brother's Keeper

1. Explain the "schizophrenic nature" of the Democratic Party in 1960. Why was the southern wing of the party so powerful? What did the southern Democrats want?

2. How did Robert Kennedy manage the touchy issue of race relations during his brother's 1960 presidential campaign? What effect did the arrest of Martin Luther King, Jr., have on the Kennedy campaign? What does it tell us about race relations in America and the role of the Kennedy brothers?

3. The telephone calls made to Coretta King and Judge Mitchell came at a critical time in the campaign (late October), and the Kennedys could have tried to avoid the issue. What does it tell you about them? Were they just seeking political gain or really acting out of principle?

4. What was the reaction from the press when John Kennedy named RFK to be attorney general? What are the primary functions of the attorney general?

5. Explain what the Kennedys meant by the "New Frontier."

6. Evaluate RFK's stance toward Cuba and Fidel Castro. Why did the Bay of Pigs invasion fail? What was the United States trying to accomplish by ousting Castro? What does this episode tell you about U.S. foreign policy? What does it say about the Kennedys?

7. Analyze the goals and tactics of the "freedom riders." What were they trying to accomplish? What was RFK's response? What was the significance of the standoff at the First Baptist Church in Montgomery, Alabama? What was Martin Luther King, Jr.'s role in the confrontation?

Chapter 5: Attorney General

1. What techniques did Robert Kennedy employ as attorney general to fight organized crime? Were these effective? What were the practices of the criminal syndicates that made them so dangerous in RFK's view?

2. What does the violence at the University of Mississippi around the admission of James Meredith tell us about the problems RFK faced in the South? What were the political forces that were the most contentious that RFK had to face down? Why did RFK want the civil rights movement to move toward voter registration? Why did he call for a "cooling off period"?

3. What does RFK's authorization of the FBI wiretap of Martin Luther King, Jr., tell us about his commitment to civil rights?

Did J. Edgar Hoover need permission from the attorney general to wiretap people? Why would RFK sign the authorization when Hoover was carrying out such activities without his signature? Evaluate Hoover's role in American history.

4. What is "counterinsurgency"? Did it work? What was RFK's view of counterinsurgency as a new weapon in the Cold War?

5. Evaluate RFK's handling of the Cuban missile crisis. What policies worked to defuse the conflict? What policies would have more than likely been disastrous if followed? What was RFK's role in the secret diplomacy? What can we learn from the Cuban missile crisis about threats from weapons of mass destruction?

6. How did Martin Luther King, Jr., attain his goal of integrating public facilities in Birmingham, Alabama, against such fierce resistance? Did King's movement press the Kennedy administration to send a civil rights bill to Congress? How did George Wallace defy the federal courts? What did the Kennedy administration have to do to push Wallace aside? What did the March on Washington accomplish?

Chapter 6: Tragedy and Rebirth

1. How did the events of November 1963 affect Robert Kennedy's political standing? How would you characterize his relationship with the new President? How did these events change American history? Why did RFK seek a seat in the U.S. Senate?

2. What can we learn from RFK's 1964 campaign against Senator Keating in New York? What kinds of voters did RFK reach out to? What were the issues in the 1964 election? What did you learn about RFK by reading about his style as a candidate?

3. What were some of RFK's early criticisms of the Johnson administration? Why was his changing stand on the Vietnam War problematic? What did RFK and his brother do in the early 1960s to expand the U.S. involvement in Vietnam? Why was the United States intervening in Vietnam's internal affairs? What was the Kennedy administration's role in the overthrow of Ngo Dinh Diem? Why was Diem ousted, and how did this decision change the political terrain in Saigon? What was RFK's role in these events?

4. How did RFK's views on Vietnam change during his first year in the U.S. Senate? Why was he beginning to oppose the

escalating American involvement? What was the substance of his prescription for a peaceful settlement? What did he think about the role of the National Liberation Front (Vietcong) in Saigon politics?

5. Did President Lyndon Johnson have bipartisan support for increasing the American involvement in fighting Communism in Vietnam? How were RFK's views on Vietnam in February 1966 received by the mainstream press and his own Democratic Party?

Chapter 7: Senator Kennedy, the Cautious Critic

1. How did Robert Kennedy's many trips abroad during his first 18 months in the U.S. Senate change his view of the world and his place in it? Explain RFK's evolution from an ardent anti-Castro zealot to an advocate of social justice in Latin America.

2. Why did RFK choose to focus on domestic issues for most of 1966? What were his views on the causes of poverty? What were his proposed solutions? Explain the general goals and practices of his development program for Bedford-Stuyvesant. Was it successful? Were RFK's ideas about poverty and relief embraced by the Johnson administration? Why or why not?

3. Describe the relationship between RFK and the United Farm Workers. Did RFK recognize UFW leader César Chávez as being a friend and political ally? Why or why not? What does RFK's work on the Subcommittee on Migrant Labor tell us about his views on labor unionism?

4. Why have RFK's words resonated so strongly with the people of South Africa? Explain the significance of his June 1966 trip to South Africa and what it tells us about racism as a global phenomenon. What did RFK accomplish by going to South Africa? What kinds of changes were taking place on the African continent at the time of RFK's visit? How did the experience affect RFK's view of the world?

5. What was the significance of the "peace feeler" incident? How did RFK's trip to Europe in February 1967 change his views of Vietnam and of the Johnson administration? What were the central ideas in RFK's "Stop the Bombing" speech?

Chapter 8: Coming Out Against the Vietnam War

1. How were the critiques of the Vietnam War articulated by Martin Luther King, Jr., and Robert Kennedy similar? How were they different? How did King's stand on Vietnam affect his standing with the Johnson administration? How did King's more moderate allies in the civil rights movement respond?

2. How did RFK's trip to the Mississippi Delta change his views on poverty in America? What did he try to do about it?

3. Why did RFK decide to close ranks politically with President Johnson at the June 1967 Democratic Party banquet in New York City? How did it play out with those who wanted RFK to take a tougher stand on the Vietnam War? What does this tell us about RFK's pragmatism and leanings toward political expediency? What was the response of the anti-war Citizens for Kennedy organizations?

4. How did the riots in Detroit during the summer of 1967 and Martin Luther King, Jr.'s Poor People's Campaign affect RFK's evolving views on poverty and race relations? What is the significance of RFK's increasingly moralistic criticisms of the Vietnam War, both during his public appearances and in *To Seek a Newer World*, the book that he published in the fall of 1967?

5. How did the Johnson administration react to RFK's stronger anti-war statements? What kinds of political problems for RFK did Minnesota Senator Eugene McCarthy cause when he entered the Democratic primary races as a peace candidate? How did RFK respond to the McCarthy candidacy?

Chapter 9: Presidential Candidate

1. What was the Tet Offensive, and how did it transform the Vietnam War? How did Robert Kennedy respond to Tet? What were the key points in RFK's interpretation of the meaning of the offensive? How did Tet change the political environment in the United States? Could the United States be "victorious" militarily in Vietnam after Tet, yet become severely weakened politically inside Vietnam? Why or why not? Why did RFK choose to give his post-Tet analysis with Chicago Mayor Richard Daley by his side?

2. How did Eugene McCarthy's strong showing in the New Hampshire primary change RFK's views about running for President and challenging President Johnson in 1968? Why did RFK enter the presidential race? Did he have a chance of winning the nomination? Did McCarthy have a chance of winning the nomination? How did the Johnson administration respond?

3. Why did RFK campaign in Alabama, Georgia, and Tennessee even though these states were not having primaries and his popularity in the South was thin? What does this action tell you about RFK's presidential bid and his campaign strategy?

4. Why did President Johnson decide not to seek his party's nomination for President in 1968? Did RFK's challenge push him in that direction? Was Johnson's presidency a failure? Why or why not? Was the Vietnam War central to his decision? Did Johnson try to pass on the presidency to his vice president, Hubert Humphrey? Did Johnson ever wish to see RFK in the White House?

Chapter 10: From Victory to Tragedy

1. How did the assassination of Martin Luther King, Jr., affect Robert Kennedy's political standing? Did RFK's speech in Indianapolis the night of King's murder prevent that city from exploding into violence? How? Evaluate RFK's extemporaneous remarks that night.

2. What do RFK's primary victories in Indiana and Nebraska tell us about his wide-ranging appeal to voters? What was he saying on the campaign trail about the war, poverty, and race relations? What kind of coalitions did RFK form to win the primaries? Where was he trying to take the nation?

3. Why did RFK lose to McCarthy in Oregon? How did he respond to being the first Kennedy to lose an election after 26 consecutive victories? How did this affect the Kennedy activists, such as César Chávez and the UFW, who were preparing for the California primary?

4. How did RFK win the California primary? What were the key groups who supported his candidacy in the Golden State? What themes and ideas did RFK put forth in his victory speech on the night of June 4, 1968? Do some of these beliefs and challenges still resonate all of these years later? What in particular did you find interesting in RFK's views and beliefs?

A Note on the Sources

Any study of Robert F. Kennedy must begin with the work of Arthur M. Schlesinger, Jr. Schlesinger, a historian who had worked for both John and Robert Kennedy, produced a magisterial 1978 biography *Robert Kennedy and His Times* (New York: Ballantine, 1978) that won a National Book Award. In *Robert Kennedy and His Times*, Schlesinger places Kennedy in his historical context, with personal insights peppered throughout its 1,107 pages. Critics have called Schlesinger a "court historian" of the Kennedys and have accused him of willfully overlooking some of the blemishes of both men's careers and characters, such as President Kennedy's infidelities and Robert Kennedy's plotting to overthrow Castro. Still *Robert Kennedy and His Times* stands as the most thorough reference work on Robert Kennedy's life.

Robert Kennedy's own works shed light on his views. His first book, *The Enemy Within: The McClellan Committee's Crusade Against Jimmy Hoffa and Corrupt Labor Unions* (New York: De Capo Press, 1960), shows he viewed his work on the committee as a "crusade." Kennedy's second book, *The Pursuit of Justice* (New York: Harper & Row, 1964), was written with the help of Theodore J. Lowi, a professor of government at Cornell University, and fleshes out his evolving ideas of society and politics. *To Seek a Newer World* (New York: Bantam, 1967) is a compilation of expanded versions of speeches on civil rights and race relations, poverty, and the war in Vietnam he wrote while serving as senator from New York. It is a book designed to clarify his positions in preparation for a possible presidential campaign. Kennedy's most famous book, *Thirteen Days: A Memoir of the Cuban Missile Crisis* (New York: W.W. Norton, 1969), was published shortly after his death. *Thirteen Days* was pulled together from his diaries during the October 1962 crisis, and it was made into a film and a television drama. It is an intimate first-hand account of the crisis.

The most important scholarly book written by a professional historian on Kennedy's life up to the time he ran for the Senate is James W. Hilty's superb work of historical biography: *Robert Kennedy: Brother Protector* (Philadelphia: Temple University Press, 1997). Hilty's work informs my chapters dealing with Kennedy's life through the attorney general period; I found his book as useful as Schlesinger's. My own study of Kennedy's Senate years—Joseph A. Palermo, *In His Own Right: The Political Odyssey of Senator Robert F. Kennedy* (New York: Columbia University Press, 2001)—has been referred to in the scholarly reviews as an important work by a professional historian that picks up the story where Hilty leaves off. I argue that the social movements of the period pressed Kennedy to take tougher stands on the Vietnam War and on social injustices and that, after hesitating for fear of the political consequences, Kennedy more often than not made the right choice.

Among the more recent works on Kennedy is Evan Thomas's *Robert Kennedy: His Life* (New York: Simon & Schuster, 2000). Thomas, a *Newsweek* magazine editor, presents a highly readable, if conventional, account of Kennedy's life, though at times his lack of training as a historian is apparent. Another recent work, Ronald Steel's *In Love with Night: The American Romance with Robert Kennedy* (New York: Simon & Schuster, 2000), is based entirely on secondary sources and not without its flaws. Steel is clearly a professional historian who is capable of writing masterful biography, as exemplified by his *Walter Lippmann and the American Century* (Boston, Massachusetts: Little, Brown, 1980). However, in his sparse study of Kennedy, Steel overstates his argument of a "romance" with Kennedy while he was alive and fails to delineate Kennedy's evolving views on the Vietnam War; he somewhat cynically concludes that Kennedy's "opposition to unilateral withdrawal and his vague formulas for a negotiated settlement hardly differed from Nixon's 'peace with honor' formula" (Steel, 2000, 194). (For an interpretation at variance with this assertion, see Palermo, 2001, chaps. 6 and 10.)

During Kennedy's lifetime, Gerald Gardner wrote a whimsical and humorous account of Kennedy's Senate campaign, *Robert Kennedy in New York: The Campaign for the Senate* (New York: Random House, 1965). Sports writer and Kennedy friend Dick Schaap's *R.F.K.* (New York: Signet, 1967) and William V. Shannon's *The Heir Apparent: Robert Kennedy and the Struggle for Power* (New York: Macmillan, 1967) both offer political and personal insights. Nick Thimmesch and William Johnson's *Robert Kennedy at 40* (New York: Norton, 1965) offers insights into Kennedy's work habits. *R.F.K.: The Man Who*

Would Be President (New York: G.P. Putnam's Sons, 1967) by Ralph de Toledano is a period piece. Sue G. Hall's edited work, *The Quotable Robert F. Kennedy* (Anderson, S.C.: Droke House, 1967), is a compilation of quotes from Kennedy with a topical index, making it a useful reference. Margaret Laing's *The Next Kennedy* (New York: Coward-McCann, 1968) is thick with style but thin on analysis; she wrote a similar short potboiler following the assassination, *Robert Kennedy* (London: Macdonald, 1968). *Robert F. Kennedy: A Biography* (New York: Meredith Press, 1968) by Henry A. Zeiger is a useful short biography. And Victor Lasky's *Robert F. Kennedy: The Myth and the Man* (New York: Trident, 1968) is a well-researched study devoid of romanticizing tendencies.

Village Voice journalist Jack Newfield, who covered Kennedy during his Senate years, produced a very useful memoir-history of his experiences with Kennedy entitled *Robert Kennedy: A Memoir* (New York: Penguin, 1969). This work gives the best account from the New Left's perspective. Legendary war correspondent and commentator David Halberstam, the author of *The Best and the Brightest* (New York: Random House, 1969), also wrote a lesser known but informative book about Kennedy, *The Unfinished Odyssey of Robert Kennedy* (New York: Random House, 1968). The most thorough and best written account of Kennedy's presidential campaign can be found in Jules Witcover's *85 Days: The Last Campaign of Robert F. Kennedy* (New York: Morrow, 1969); Witcover traveled with the candidate and captures the feeling of the time period. A useful compilation of essays can be found in *American Journey: The Times of Robert Kennedy* (New York: Harcourt Brace Jovanovich, 1970), edited by Kennedy partisans Jean Stein and George Plimpton.

Another earlier work that is often overlooked but that has important details found nowhere else is *On His Own: Robert F. Kennedy 1964–1968* (New York: Doubleday, 1970), written by Milton Gwirtzman and William Vanden Heuvel, two lawyers who worked with Kennedy. Edwin Guthman, Kennedy's confidante and former press secretary when he was attorney general, wrote *We Band of Brothers* (New York: Harper & Row, 1971), which is a highly personalized and sympathetic account of his experiences with the Kennedys. Later Guthman edited compilations of Kennedy's speeches with Jeffrey Schulman, *Robert Kennedy: In His Own Words* (New York: Bantam, 1988), and with Richard C. Allen, *RFK: Collected Speeches* (New York: Viking, 1993). *Of Kennedy and Kings: Making Sense of the Sixties* (New York: Farrar, 1980) by Kennedy's friend Harris Wofford presents some unique insights, especially relating to the civil rights movement. David Burner and Thomas West's *The Torch Is Passed: The Kennedy*

Brothers and American Liberalism (New York: Antheneum, 1984) is a sympathetic account with a description of what the authors call "Kennedy Liberalism." Lester David and Irene David, in *Bobby Kennedy: The Making of a Folk Hero* (New York: Dodd, 1986), offer an informal, gossipy account of RFK's career that is surprisingly well researched and factual.

Warren Rogers, a journalist friend of RFK who was present at the Ambassador Hotel the night he was shot, produced an engaging and descriptive work, *When I Think of Bobby: A Personal Memoir of the Kennedy Years* (New York: HarperPerennial, 1993). Brian Dooley, in *Robert Kennedy: The Final Years* (Staffordshire, England: Keele University Press, 1995), offers a concise secondary-source biography of the 1965–1968 period. Paul Henggeler's *The Kennedy Persuasion: The Politics of Style Since JFK* (Chicago: Ivan Dee, 1995) is useful for its political insights. Jeff Shesol's *Mutual Contempt: Lyndon Johnson, Robert Kennedy, and the Feud That Defined a Decade* (New York: Norton, 1997) is an excellent account of the personal rivalry between RFK and LBJ; it is well researched but thin on social history and analysis. Helen O'Donnell, the wife of Kennedy family friend Kenneth O'Donnell, in *A Common Good: The Friendship of Robert F. Kennedy and Kenneth P. O'Donnell* (New York: William Morrow, 1998), offers anecdotes that could come only from a close personal friend. Arlene Schulman authored *Robert F. Kennedy: Promise for the Future* (New York: Facts on File, 1998), a brief biography geared for students. Kennedy's son Maxwell Taylor Kennedy edited a work entitled *Make Gentle the Life of This World* (New York: Harcourt, 1998) that combines photographs and RFK's words relating to a breadth of topics. In *The Last Patrician: Bobby Kennedy and the End of American Aristocracy* (New York: St. Martin's, 1998), Michael Knox Beran overstates his case that RFK's legacy is conservative. Richard Mahoney's *Sons and Brothers: The Days of Jack and Bobby Kennedy* (New York: Arcade, 1999) is a good overview of RFK's life.

Konstantin Sidorenko's *Robert F. Kennedy: A Spiritual Biography* (New York: Crossroads, 2000) focuses on the more personal stories of RFK's life. Kennedy's former legislative aide Peter Edelman, in *Searching for America's Heart: RFK and the Renewal of Hope* (New York: Houghton Mifflin, 2001), gives an account of current social policies that RFK would have probably embraced. W. J. Rorabough places Kennedy in the context of the culture of the 1960s in *Kennedy and the Promise of the Sixties* (Cambridge, U.K.: Cambridge University Press, 2002); and David Talbot's superb *Brothers: The Hidden History of the Kennedy Years* (New York: Free Press, 2007) is a well-researched study of RFK's thoughts on the events of November 1963.

For the 1960s, civil rights, and RFK's role, books of interest that I list here based on their usefulness to this project include Taylor Branch's trilogy: *Parting the Waters: America in the King Years, 1953–1963* (New York: Simon & Schuster, 1988), *Pillar of Fire: America in the King Years, 1963–1965* (New York: Simon & Schuster, 1998), and *At Canaan's Edge: America in the King Years, 1965–1968* (New York: Simon & Schuster, 2005). I also drew upon Robert Weisbrot, *Freedom Bound: A History of America's Civil Rights Movement* (New York: Plume, 1990); James M. Washington, ed., *A Testament of Hope: The Essential Writings and Speeches of Martin Luther King, Jr.* (New York: HarperCollins, 1986); David Garrow, *Bearing the Cross: Martin Luther King, Jr. and the Southern Christian Leadership Conference* (New York: Vintage, 1986); Clayborne Carson, *In Struggle: SNCC and the Black Awakening of the 1960s* (Cambridge: Harvard University Press, 1981); Henry Hampton et al., *Voices of Freedom: An Oral History of the Civil Rights Movement from the 1950s Through the 1980s* (New York: Bantam, 1990); Martin Luther King, Jr., *Where Do We Go from Here? Chaos or Community?* (Boston: Beacon, 1967); Gerald Horne, *Fire This Time: The Watts Uprising and the 1960s* (Charlottesville, Virginia: University Press of Virginia, 1995); Charles Evers, *Have No Fear: The Charles Evers Story* (New York: Wiley, 1997); Kenneth O'Reilly, ed., *Black Americans: The FBI Files* (New York: Carroll & Graff, 1994); Kenneth O'Reilly, *"Racial Matters": The FBI's Secret File on Black America, 1960–1972* (New York: Free Press, 1989); Robert Mann, *The Walls of Jericho: Lyndon Johnson, Hubert Humphrey, Richard Russell and the Struggle for Civil Rights* (New York: Harcourt Brace, 1996); and Raymond Arsenault's *Freedom Riders: 1961 and the Struggle for Racial Justice* (Oxford University Press, 2006).

General works on the period and biographies include Robert Dallek, *An Unfinished Life: John F. Kennedy, 1917–1963* (New York: Little, Brown, 2003), *Hail to the Chief: The Making and Unmaking of American Presidents* (New York: Hyperion, 1996), and *Flawed Giant: Lyndon Johnson and His Times 1961–1973* (Oxford: Oxford University Press, 1998); William Chafe, *Never Stop Running* (New York: HarperCollins, 1993); Dan Carter, *The Politics of Rage: George Wallace, the Origins of the New Conservatism, and the Transformation of American Politics* (New York: Simon & Schuster, 1995); Charles DeBenedetti, *An American Ordeal: The Antiwar Movement in the Vietnam Era* (Syracuse, New York: Syracuse University Press, 1990); Eric Foner, *The Story of American Freedom* (New York: Norton, 1998); James Giglio, *The Presidency of John F. Kennedy* (Lawrence, Kansas: University of Kansas Press, 1991);

Terry Anderson, *The Movement and the Sixties* (Oxford: Oxford University Press, 1995); Irving Bernstein, *Guns and Butter: The Presidency of Lyndon Johnson* (Oxford: Oxford University Press, 1996); Michael Beschloss, *Taking Charge: The Johnson White House Tapes, 1963–1964* (New York: Simon & Schuster, 1997); Paul Conkin, *Big Daddy from the Pedernales: Lyndon Baines Johnson* (Boston: Twayne, 1986); Doug Dowd, *Blues for America: A Critique, a Lament, and Some Memories* (New York: Monthly Review, 1997); Arthur Matasow, *The Unraveling of America: A History of Liberalism in the 1960s* (New York: Harper & Row, 1984); Todd Gitlin, *The Sixties: Years of Hope, Days of Rage* (New York: Bantam, 1987); Jon Margolis, *The Last Innocent Year: America in 1964: The Beginning of the "Sixties"* (New York: Morrow, 1999); Richard Goodwin, *Remembering America: A Voice from the Sixties* (New York: Harper & Row, 1988); Charles Kaiser, *1968 in America: Music, Politics, Counterculture, and the Shaping of a Generation* (New York: Weidenfeld, 1988); Gerald Howard, ed., *The Sixties: The Art, Attitudes, Politics, and Media of Our Most Explosive Decade* (New York: Marlowe, 1991); Doris Kearns Goodwin, *Lyndon Johnson and the American Dream* (New York: Harper & Row, 1976); William Leuchtenburg, *Under the Shadow of FDR: From Harry Truman to Ronald Reagan* (Ithaca, New York: Cornell University Press, 1983); James Miller, *Democracy in the Streets: From Port Huron to the Siege of Chicago* (Cambridge: Harvard University Press, 1987); Herbert Parmet, *JFK: The Presidency of John Kennedy* (New York: Dial, 1983); Tom Wells, *The War Within: America's Battle over Vietnam* (New York: Holt, 1994); David Burner, *Making Peace with the 60s* (Princeton, New Jersey: Princeton University Press, 1996); Mark Hamilton Lytle, *America's Uncivil Wars: The Sixties Era from Elvis to the Fall of Richard Nixon* (Oxford: Oxford University Press, 2006); and Howard Zinn, *A Power Governments Cannot Suppress* (San Francisco: City Lights, 2007).

Books on the assassination that are essential reading include Philip H. Melanson, *The Robert F. Kennedy Assassination: New Revelations on the Conspiracy and Cover-Up* (New York: Shapolsky, 1991); William Turner and John Christian, *The Assassination of Robert F. Kennedy: The Conspiracy and Coverup* (New York: Thunder's Mouth Press, 1978, 1993); Francine Klagsbrun and David Whitney, eds., *Assassination: Robert F. Kennedy 1925–1968* (New York: Cowles, 1968); Robert Houghton, *Special Unit Senator: The Investigation of the Assassination of Senator Robert F. Kennedy* (New York: Random House, 1970); and Dan Moldea, *The Killing of Robert F. Kennedy: An Investigation of Motive, Means, and Opportunity* (New York: Norton, 1995).

Other works I consulted include Ernest May and Philip Zelikow, eds., *The Kennedy Tapes: Inside the White House During the Cuban Missile Crisis* (Cambridge: Harvard University Press, 1997); George McT. Kahin, *Intervention: How America Became Involved in Vietnam* (New York: Alfred A. Knopf, 1986); Robert Weisbrot, *Maximum Danger: Kennedy, the Missiles, and the Crisis of American Confidence* (Chicago, Illinois: Ivan R. Dee, 2001); Marvin Gettelman et al., eds., *Vietnam and America: The Most Comprehensive Documented History of the Vietnam War* (New York: Grove, 1995); Robert McNamara, *In Retrospect: The Tragedy and Lessons of Vietnam* (New York: Times Books, 1995); Marilyn Young, *The Vietnam Wars, 1945–1990* (New York: HarperPerennial, 1991); William Rust, *Kennedy in Vietnam: American Vietnam Policy 1960–1963* (New York: Da Capo, 1985); Brian VanDeMark, *Into the Quagmire: Lyndon Johnson and the Escalation of the Vietnam War* (Oxford: Oxford University Press, 1995); Christian Appy, *Working-Class War: American Combat Soldiers in Vietnam* (Chapel Hill, N.C.: University of North Carolina Press, 1993); Larry Berman, *Lyndon Johnson's War: The Road to Stalemate* (New York: Norton, 1989); Peter Braestrup, *Big Story: How the American Press and Television Reported and Interpreted the Crisis of Tet in Vietnam and Washington* (Boulder, Colo.: Westview, 1977); Robert Buzzanco, *Masters of War: Military Dissent and Politics in the Vietnam Era* (Oxford: Oxford University Press, 1996); Daniel Ellsberg, *Papers on the War* (New York: Simon & Schuster, 1972); *Pentagon Papers,* Senator Gravel ed. (Boston: Beacon, 1970); Don Oberdorfer, *Tet! The Turning Point in the Vietnam War* (New York: Doubleday, 1971); Neil Sheehan, *A Bright Shining Lie: John Paul Vann and America in Vietnam* (New York: Vintage, 1988); Ronald Spector, *After Tet: The Bloodiest Year of the War* (New York: Free Press, 1985); Andrew Rotter, *The Light at the End of the Tunnel: A Vietnam War Anthology* (New York: St. Martin's Press, 1991); Patrick Hearden, *The Tragedy of Vietnam* (New York: Pearson Longman, 2005); Walter LaFeber, *America, Russia, and the Cold War, 1945–2006* (New York: McGraw-Hill, 2006); Gareth Porter, *Perils of Dominance: Imbalance of Power and the Road to War in Vietnam* (Berkeley: University of California Press, 2005); and Frederick Logevil, *Choosing War: The Lost Chance for Peace and the Escalation of War in Vietnam* (Berkely, California: University of California Press, 1999).

Index